# THINK FIT **METHOD**
## JOURNAL & DEVOTIONAL

A journey of self discovery that will reunite you with your best self
by conquering mindset on the road to your health and wellness

## JENNY MIRE

THINK FIT METHOD DEEPER DIVE BIBLE STUDY BY DEBBIE HEISER

# ALL RIGHTS RESERVED

THIS JOURNAL BELONGS TO:

NAME:

_____

CONTACT INFO:

_____

CONGRATULATIONS ON MAKING THE INVESTMENT
IN YOUR HEALTH AND HEALING YOUR MIND.

I am so excited for the journey you are on
and look forward to hearing what
God does in your life over the next couple of months.

*Jenny*

IT'S NOT

WHO YOU

ARE THAT

HOLDS YOU BACK,

IT'S WHO

YOU THINK

YOU ARE NOT.

# SET YOUR GOALS

What are your goals for this journal?

What future do you want to create for yourself?

What has to change for you to make that a reality?

List your top 5 goals for the next 8 weeks

YOUR WORTH. YOUR WHY.

1

# WEEK ONE

*B*efore we dive in to unpacking your why, you must know your worth and truly believe you are worth it.

Worth. Value. Belonging. These words have something in common, don't they? It's likely that at least one of these words pulls at your heartstrings a little bit. Why? Because every single human longs to know they have worth, they are valuable and they belong. I say this because we were made by a loving Father who wants and pursues us even when we don't recognize it. Because we are created and intricately crafted to share a relationship with Him and others. And in my humble opinion, I believe it's fair to go on the record stating that we will struggle with seeing ourselves as worthy, believing we have value and have a place of belonging when we don't consider the price paid for us by our loving creator. We will struggle when we let the negative and discouraging and even ugly thoughts bounce around in our minds and become the rhetoric we become accustomed to hearing and believing day in and day out. We beat ourselves up. We negative self talk, we allow our struggles to define us and sometimes we believe the lie that God couldn't love us because we fail and we sin and it's all just too much. I'm just going to cut straight to the heart of it— we forget what the word of God says about us. We forget that His atonement, His sacrifice takes all of it and separates our mess as far as the east is from the west. His grace covers every speck of dirt that we carry with us. And it's so amazing, it's so rich with love and mercy that we struggle to fathom how loved we truly are.

*We forget about our freedom in Christ.*

*We forget that he created us and chases us and beckons us home..*

*We forget that when he looks at us, he sees his son, he sees Jesus living in us and that is good.*

It doesn't have to be that way though. There is a better way. Friends, our worth is immeasurable- and it's because we have a God that loves us unconditionally. A Father who says "come to me" and find who you were created to be. I am for you. We run to every other "thing" to fill the void in our hearts and we wonder why we feel "less than." The only way to remedy this hole and hurt is to start believing what God says. He wants to be in a relationship with you and He wants to heal your heart. How can we start believing we have value and are worthy when we feel anything but? Let's start at the source...

*Psalms 139:13-15 tells us:*

*"For you formed my inward parts; you knitted me together in my mother's womb. I will give thanks to You, for I am fearfully and wonderfully made; Wonderful are your works; and my soul knows it very well. My frame was not hidden from you, when I was being made in secret, and skillfully wrought in the depths of the earth."*

God says these things about you. Fearfully made. Wonderfully made. KNOWN from the very beginning. This is a picture of true, unyielding love that has no parameters and has no caveat, the one requirement to access it: Come to Jesus and surrender your life to Him, claim Him as Lord of your life. What a savior! What a sovereign and beautiful God we serve. That He would send His son to the cross so that we could live with the hope each day that we are loved, unconditionally and forever.

We hold ourselves to such a high standard, we never shut off our brains. We struggle sometimes to believe that we could be loved because we have a hard time loving ourselves. We measure ourselves against often self imposed, unrealistic standards and ideas that can hold us captive and fog the clear voice of Jesus that says, just come to me. Live in the freedom and hope and promise that He has us in the palm of His hand and He could not love you more than He already does.

## THE BIBLE IS FILLED WITH THIS PROMISE IN 1ST JOHN 4:16

"So we have come to know and to believe the love that God has for us. God is love, and whoever abides in love abides in God, and God abides in him."

Stop for a minute to savor and relish this deep love and to let it wash over you— shake off everything else, every detail and pursuit and know that you are loved 100% right now, who you are, where you are and start believing He couldn't want you more tomorrow than He does today. Maybe you know this, or maybe it's the first time you've heard this promise. You are loved. You have worth and value and you having belonging in Christ. It's not a performance game or a conditional thing. It's free and it's good and right now, even as you read this, He looks at you with daddy's eyes. You are favored, dear one. So let's start living that way, as favored children who are conquerors. I challenge you to start even now, shifting your focus from negative to the refreshing truth that you are worthy, valuable and loved and have been every day of your life. To shift your negatives to the attitude of a conqueror. Let's end on that thought and with this encouragement from the book of Romans.

*"No, in all these things we are more than conquerors through Him who loved us.
For I am sure that neither death nor life, nor angels nor rulers, nor things present
nor things to come, nor powers, nor height nor depth, nor anything else in all
creation, will be able to separate us from the love of God in Christ Jesus our Lord."*
*Romans 8:37-39*

You are worthy. You are valuable. You belong and you are loved. Now, let's start living in that promise.

Your worth comes from God. So let me ask you, do you feel you are worth it? Do you feel you are worth the time it will take to reset your mind? Do you feel you are worth the effort to stop emotional eating?

Let's answer some key questions today. Head over to worksheet 1:1 and complete it. Now that you believe you are worth it and you are worth this process of healing your inside and outside, let's dive in to identifying your why.

I truly believe that in order to reach your goals, you must dig deep and figure out WHY you want to reach those goals. More often than not when asked why someone wants to be healthier they either want to lose x number of lbs or they want to "look better" on the outside. But if this is as deep as it gets for you, then what will be the driving force that gets you out of bed when your motivation runs out?

Finding your true WHY is going to be the driving force of your success. It is impossible to stay committed and reach your goals when you don't know your deep down why. Not just the surface why, but the deep down driving force of why you want to be healthy. Your why is the real reason - the underlying reason - you want to change. This becomes your core driver and motivator when motivation lacks.

When your why is identified and becomes a part of your core being and aligns with your intentions, you will be unstoppable. Once you get to the root of your why, it will change you. It will be the thing that gets you out of bed in the morning when you so badly don't want to.

Discovering your why is going to be the thing that changes this for you. It is the most important step to reaching your goals after finally believing you are worth it. However, finding your deep down why is not always easy. Over the past year, I have been diving in to my own why on many levels with the help of one of my mentors, and let me tell you, it is hard but it is so worth it once you finally dial it in.

If you are ready to make a change and stop making excuses, then let's get down to it. Let's work hard on finding your WHY!

When working through your why, there is no wrong answer, however, it needs to be personal to YOU. It needs to be something that will keep you going when it gets hard. Yes, you want to feel better... but WHY do you want to feel better? Yes, you want to look better in your clothes... but WHY do you want to look better in your clothes? Yes, you want to overcome illness... but WHY do you want to overcome illness? Is it because you want to not hurt anymore? Is it because you want to have the energy for your kids without the aches and pains? What is it? Once you find that why, the excuses will fade away and you will look for solutions instead!

To find your deep down WHY, head over to worksheet 1:2 on page 12 and complete.

YOUR WORTH COMES FROM GOD.

So let me ask you, do you feel you are worth it? Do you feel you are worth the time it will take to reset your mind? Do you feel you are worth the effort to stop emotional eating?

RESOURCES:
NASB Thinline Bible. (2002). Grand Rapids, Mich.: Zondervan.

# Self Worth

**Are you worth it?**

**Write this statement: "I am worth it."**

**Why I am worth it?**
List 5 things that make YOU worth this process.

**Write this statement: "I love myself."**

**What do I love about myself?**
List 5 things you love about yourself.

1.

2.

3.

4.

5.

Who am I worth it to? (hint: your Creator, yourself, your family)

How do others see me?

How do I see myself?

THINK FIT METHOD *tip*

Stand in front of a mirror and tell yourself OUT LOUD that you are worth it.
**REPEAT THIS 5 TIMES.**

Now close your eyes and in your mind's eye visualize the words "I am worth it."
**REPEAT THIS FOR 2 MINUTES.**

# Finding Your Why

This worksheet is from Debbie Heiser of Three Vines Consulting, LLC and was adapted from a magazine article.

**What's your objective? Why do you want it? But why? Why? Why?**

**What's your objective?** (ie: I want to be active 260 days out of the year or 5 days a week)

**Why do you want it?** (ie: So I can fit into some of the clothes I have in my closet.)

**But why?** (ie: So when I go back for my high school reunion I can feel confident.)

**Why?** (ie: So I can feel happier and lighter.)

Why? (ie: Because I'm tired of getting out of bed every morning aching and hurting.)

Your own road map might take fewer or more WHYS. The point is to keep asking until you arrive at your ultimate reason. When you have found it, hang it up in front of you or create a vision board!

# Weekly Reflection

What were the biggest revelations and lessons learned this week?

What are you grateful for this past week?

List three positives of the week when it comes to your nutrition and exercise journey:

List three things you would like to improve on next week.
What concrete actions can you take to work towards these?

1.

2.

3.

When did you show yourself you are worth it this week? List as many as applicable:

From 1-10, how do you feel you did this week?

From 1-10, how do you feel you did this week?

What does Psalms 139:13-15 mean to you this week?

> *"For you formed my inward parts; you knitted me together in my mother's womb. I praise you, for I am fearfully and wonderfully made. Wonderful are your works; my soul knows it very well. My frame was not hidden from you, when I was being made in secret, intricately woven in the depths of the earth."*

How can you apply this verse moving forward on this journey?

# WEEK ONE DEVOTIONS

Psalms 139:1-5

[1]You have searched me, Lord, and you know me.

[2] You know when I sit and when I rise;

you perceive my thoughts from afar.

[3] You discern my going out and my lying down;

you are familiar with all my ways.

[4] Before a word is on my tongue you, Lord, know it

completely. [5] You hem me in behind and before, and

you lay your hand upon me.

*W*elcome to the Think Fit Method Deeper Dive Bible Study. This study is designed to provide study, prayer, reflection, and exercises to help clarify what God is bringing to light for you. Part of the study works on the inner game, while other parts focus on the outer plans to help aid you on your journey. Spend as much or as little time as you like, the material is for you to use as you see fit. Best results come with a quiet place, a journal or something to write on and your Bible for reference.

**A word of wisdom:** Be kind to yourself and allow God to reveal what you need right when you need it. I don't know about you, but when I try to force God's plan into my will or I sit back and don't pay attention – well, let's just say it's not all good! Those times when I have been patient, listened and continued, sometimes moment by moment to seek God's will, I am constantly in awe of how life comes together in a beautiful tapestry.

**Format:** The study will include multiple bible verses focused on the eight-week Think Fit Method topics with questions to work through. Be open to things that come up and **utilize a journal** to write down even what may seem as random thoughts. The Going Deep sections will include exercises and additional resources you may find helpful!

My hope and prayer for you as you work through the Think Fit Method and supplement with this study is that you experience the deep and abiding peace and love of God! Blessings

## WEEK 1: YOUR WORTH. YOUR WHY.

Psalms 139 is packed with great stuff that we will be looking at throughout the program! Take a moment to read the entire passage and note how many times David states that God knows us! (Hint: he might use other words than know, such as discern, perceive, etc.)

**Read verses 1 – 6:** How wonderful is this sisters and brothers? God knows us...every random and what we think are insignificant thoughts or movements, He knows. How refreshing to remove the masks we hide in and bare ourselves to Him – BECAUSE HE ALREADY KNOWS. Now don't get me wrong, I know sometimes the hardest part is that we need to move from denial into realizing God does know it already! When I mentioned baring yourself to God...anyone find that a bit frightening?

If so, don't judge the fear, take a moment and **pray** for God to reveal why baring yourself to Him might create fear and where the root of the fear may be coming from. When we identify these fears, it allows us to get rid of them.

- How do verses 1-6 resonate with you?
- Do you feel fear?
- What is the fear and where might it be coming from?

Remember, becoming aware of our fears diminishes fear's power because it has entered the light and is not hidden. Once you have become aware, turn it over to God! Utilize your journal to jot down some thoughts, prayers and notes for continued reflection.

Fear of being authentic or vulnerable usually is tied to self-worth. Many people ask the following questions: Am I worth being loved? I am worth treating my body well? Do I love myself when I look in the mirror or is all I see negative? Take a minute and reflect on these questions. When do you find yourself being critical? Utilize your **journal** to note anything that comes to your awareness.

## Going Deep

*As negative thoughts come into your mind about your worth, change the thoughts into a phrase of affirmation. For examples, "My upper thighs rub together and are huge" Change this to an affirmation statement. "My upper thighs provide me the ability to walk, do a squat and help me as a foundation of movement in my lower body". This might sound quirky, but it works! Later in this journal, Jenny will have you do a similar exercise. Why repeat it? Because our brains create patterns, in this case some patterns we want to change. Practicing the art of finding the silver lining is an important step to shifting patterns!*

**When we doubt we are worth love, it also makes it difficult to love others.** Luke 10:27 (NIV) says, "Love the Lord your God with all your HEART, and with all your SOUL, with all your STRENGTH and with all your MIND and love your neighbor as yourself." How do you love your neighbor (others) today? Do you find yourself tired, worn out and frustrated when you are asked to love yourself? Can you come up with any excuse to not love yourself? It is so important to remember God asks us to love others, but friends, I think we overlook an important part. He asks us to love others AS WE LOVE OURSELVES. **Meditate** on that for a bit and **utilize your journal** to make note of any awareness that arises.

Now take a moment to **pray** for God's guidance in this next activity. Look at yourself and how you treat others. Make a list in your **journal** of generalities and specific ways you have loved others in your life. Now, let's shift the focus to you. How do you love yourself? You may start out with outer game rituals or special "treats" you provide yourself such as a massage once a quarter, or a coffee date with a friend however really lean into this exercise. How do you show love and respect to yourself? (Please make notes in your **journal** as we will refer to these in later studies.)

Taking care of ourselves, loving ourselves, our minds, hearts, bodies and souls allows us to take care of and love others in our lives. "The most difficult part of teaching people to respect and listen to their bodies is overcoming their conviction that there is nothing to respect" (Roth, 2010, p. 64) Refer back to Worksheet 1:1 on page 10. What is it that makes you feel worth going through this process? What do you love about yourself? How does this allow you to show love to others?

Just as critical as understanding and accepting our worth, is understanding the intention behind changing behaviors. Why are you wanting to change? As you work through the worksheets provided, each level will draw you into a deeper intention. Lean into this and really allow yourself to dig deep. Many times starting out with your why motivates you and then you realize there is even a deeper reason. In some cases, the why might change, morph or do a 360 as you change!

> ## Going Deep
>
> *Ask 5 other people who you feel safe with, care about or respect what they love about you. Compare their answers to those that you wrote in the "How do others see me?" in Worksheet 1:1 on page 10. Jot down the answers and any insights you have in your journal and keep them for continued reference.*

God provides us knowledge that He has plans for us. **Read Jeremiah 29:11-13**. God does not want us bound by chains of doubt or low self-esteem. He rather wants us to prosper. Prosperity isn't always tied to financial definitions. Think about this friend – He wants to give you victory and success in your health journey. Our bodies are a temple to allow us to do the good works he has called us to do! Keep in mind finding the why is not necessarily adding something but removing something. Go back and review the worksheet you completed. **Pray and meditate** over your intentions. As you work through the program, note those NSV (Non-Scale Victories) as each of these are important steps and ways God is showing you prosperity!

As you delve deeper into God's plan be cautious to not let pride take over. Beth Moore, in her Breaking Free study explains that "People crave a human worth worshipping. We are wise not to deliver" (p16). Take some time to **pray** asking God to open your mind, body, spirit and heart to what he has in store for you through this program. Take some time to **meditate**, listening for his direction. Utilize your **journal** to make note of your heart's thoughts.

Resources:
Moore, B. (1999). Breaking free. Nashville: Adult Ministry Publishing
Roth, G. (2010). Women, food and God. New York: Scribner.
Cornerstone Bible Publishers. (1999). The Holy Bible. Nashville, Tenn.

*Journal it!*

_____

_____

_____

_____

_____

_____

_____

_____

_____

_____

_____

_____

_____

_____

_____

_____

_____

_____

_____

_____

_____

_____

_____

_____

_____

_____

_____

If you are in need of a workout plan or nutrition guidance, please jump in to my next virtual bootcamp at jennymire.com or take advantage of the full Think Fit Method portal at thinkfitmethod.com

# **MONDAY** - TRACK YOUR WORKOUT

Exercise: _____

*Rate how you feel*

| Before Workout: | 1 | 2 | 3 | 4 | 5 | 6 | 7 | 8 | 9 | 10 |
|---|---|---|---|---|---|---|---|---|---|---|

| During Workout: | 1 | 2 | 3 | 4 | 5 | 6 | 7 | 8 | 9 | 10 |
|---|---|---|---|---|---|---|---|---|---|---|

| After Workout: | 1 | 2 | 3 | 4 | 5 | 6 | 7 | 8 | 9 | 10 |
|---|---|---|---|---|---|---|---|---|---|---|

Total exercise time: _____     Approximate Calories Burned: _____

Water Goal (oz): _____     Water Consumed (oz): _____

*Today My Win Was:* _____

*Tomorrow I Will:* _____

# **TUESDAY** - TRACK YOUR WORKOUT

Exercise: _____

*Rate how you feel*

| Before Workout: | 1 | 2 | 3 | 4 | 5 | 6 | 7 | 8 | 9 | 10 |
|---|---|---|---|---|---|---|---|---|---|---|

| During Workout: | 1 | 2 | 3 | 4 | 5 | 6 | 7 | 8 | 9 | 10 |
|---|---|---|---|---|---|---|---|---|---|---|

| After Workout: | 1 | 2 | 3 | 4 | 5 | 6 | 7 | 8 | 9 | 10 |
|---|---|---|---|---|---|---|---|---|---|---|

Total exercise time: _____     Approximate Calories Burned: _____

Water Goal (oz): _____     Water Consumed (oz): _____

*Today My Win Was:* _____

*Tomorrow I Will:* _____

# WEDNESDAY - TRACK YOUR WORKOUT

Exercise: _____

*Rate how you feel*

| Before Workout: | 1 | 2 | 3 | 4 | 5 | 6 | 7 | 8 | 9 | 10 |
|---|---|---|---|---|---|---|---|---|---|---|
| During Workout: | 1 | 2 | 3 | 4 | 5 | 6 | 7 | 8 | 9 | 10 |
| After Workout: | 1 | 2 | 3 | 4 | 5 | 6 | 7 | 8 | 9 | 10 |

Total exercise time: _____   Approximate Calories Burned: _____

Water Goal (oz): _____   Water Consumed (oz): _____

*Today My Win Was:* _____

*Tomorrow I Will:* _____

# THURSDAY - TRACK YOUR WORKOUT

Exercise: _____

*Rate how you feel*

| Before Workout: | 1 | 2 | 3 | 4 | 5 | 6 | 7 | 8 | 9 | 10 |
|---|---|---|---|---|---|---|---|---|---|---|
| During Workout: | 1 | 2 | 3 | 4 | 5 | 6 | 7 | 8 | 9 | 10 |
| After Workout: | 1 | 2 | 3 | 4 | 5 | 6 | 7 | 8 | 9 | 10 |

Total exercise time: _____   Approximate Calories Burned: _____

Water Goal (oz): _____   Water Consumed (oz): _____

*Today My Win Was:* _____

*Tomorrow I Will:* _____

# **FRIDAY** - TRACK YOUR WORKOUT

Exercise: _____

*Rate how you feel*

| Before Workout: | 1 | 2 | 3 | 4 | 5 | 6 | 7 | 8 | 9 | 10 |
|---|---|---|---|---|---|---|---|---|---|---|

| During Workout: | 1 | 2 | 3 | 4 | 5 | 6 | 7 | 8 | 9 | 10 |
|---|---|---|---|---|---|---|---|---|---|---|

| After Workout: | 1 | 2 | 3 | 4 | 5 | 6 | 7 | 8 | 9 | 10 |
|---|---|---|---|---|---|---|---|---|---|---|

Total exercise time: ___    Approximate Calories Burned: ___

Water Goal (oz): ___    Water Consumed (oz): ___

*Today My Win Was:* _____

*Tomorrow I Will:* _____

# **WEEKEND** - TRACK YOUR WORKOUT

Exercise: _____

*Rate how you feel*

| Before Workout: | 1 | 2 | 3 | 4 | 5 | 6 | 7 | 8 | 9 | 10 |
|---|---|---|---|---|---|---|---|---|---|---|

| During Workout: | 1 | 2 | 3 | 4 | 5 | 6 | 7 | 8 | 9 | 10 |
|---|---|---|---|---|---|---|---|---|---|---|

| After Workout: | 1 | 2 | 3 | 4 | 5 | 6 | 7 | 8 | 9 | 10 |
|---|---|---|---|---|---|---|---|---|---|---|

Total exercise time: ___    Approximate Calories Burned: ___

Water Goal (oz): ___    Water Consumed (oz): ___

*Today My Win Was:* _____

*Tomorrow I Will:* _____

YOUR MIND

2

# WEEK TWO

# YOUR MIND

Y ou've heard it before and now you're going to hear it again. Mindset is key to anything. But why?

Mindset is the catalyst for success or failure, especially when it comes to staying committed, consistent and believing in a process, or even believing in ourselves.

Mindset, in short, is a set of beliefs or thoughts that can, in total, be summarized by saying the following about ourselves: "I can do this" or "I can't do this." It is your belief set about yourself and it's what helps you or hinders you. This could be how you view your intelligence all the way to how you view and what you believe about your body. By identifying that you are indeed worth it, you are now able to really dive in and work on resetting your mindset.

Did you know your mind determines everything? It's your brain that tells you to get up and workout and to stop eating when you aren't hungry. It's your brain that tells you that you can do this or you can't do this.

But did you know that you have the ability to control your brain? God gave you the ability to change your mindset.

*Have you ever heard the term, "You are what you eat?" Well, today I want you to know that you are what you believe you are.*

The most successful people all have something in common - they visualized and believed they could get to where they wanted to go. They imagined that they would be successful, no matter what area of life.

Your mindset is a lot more powerful than you give it credit for being. Our frame of mind can work for us and against us. In the same way a positive mindset can help us in life, a negative frame of mind can also be detrimental to us. When we focus on the negative we will struggle. It's the "garbage in, garbage out" concept. What we put in our mind has the ability to impact how we live and the kind of results we achieve or fall short on. This is why it's so so important to have positive voices in our lives and in our minds to help us fill up on good and affirming things that will be a catalyst for a "can do" attitude.

One of the biggest things on your health and fitness journey, whether you are trying to lose weight or not, is shifting your mindset. We can't change our outside without changing our inside.

I love the concept of the "Ten Principles to Change Your Brain and Your Body" by Dr. Daniel G. Amen in his book Change Your Brain, Change Your Body.  He states those ten principles are:

1. Your brain is involved in everything you do.
2. When your brain works right, your body looks and feels better. When your brain is troubled, you have trouble with how you look and feel.
3. The brain is the most complex organ in the universe. Respect it.
4. Your brain is very soft and housed in a really hard skull. Protect it.
5. The brain has only so much reserve. The more reserve you have, the healthier you are. The less reserve, the more vulnerable you are.
6. Specific parts of your brain are involved in certain behaviors. Trouble in specific parts of your brain tends to cause certain behavior problems. Understanding your brain can help you optimize it.
7. Many things hurt the brain and make it harder for you to get the body you've always wanted. Many things help the brain and make it easier to get and keep a body you love.
8. Brain imaging gives great insight into healing the brain so you can have a better body.
9. One prescription does not work for everyone - we are all unique, and you need to understand how your own personal brain functions.
10. Yes, you can change your brain and body!

I just love everything about this because it is TRUE my friends. Your brain (MINDSET) can control whether you can reach your goals. A healthier mindset will make it so much easier for you to reach your wellness goals. Never underestimate the power of thought. Everything we do in life starts with ONE thought. Your mind is a powerful thing.

Now I want you to head over to worksheet 2:1 on page 30 and complete it.
Well, in Romans 12:2 it states, "and do not be conformed to this world, but be transformed by the renewing of your mind, so that you may prove what the will of God is, that which is good and acceptable and perfect."

And again, in 1 Peter 1:13, "Therefore, prepare your minds for action, keep sober in spirit, fix your hope completely on the grace to be brought to you at the revelation of Jesus Christ."

Sometimes things that happen in our minds are not reality. And sometimes thoughts will sneak into our minds that are not our own and you must know that you do NOT have to claim these thoughts. Satan will try to get his way in our minds and will try to make us believe something that is not true of us. Now your job is going to have to be to recognize this and take those thoughts captive, giving them to Jesus.

*The first thing to do in the attempts to change your mindset is recognize that your mind has a lot of control over you.*

A popular therapy called "Cognitive Behavioral Therapy" is influenced by the belief that thoughts influence feelings which then influence behavior. So basically, you start to behave and feel as if those negative self thoughts are true. So these negative thoughts end up being father to our actions and then what we "think" turns into how we behave, how we respond and how we live out our lives.

So let me ask you, what do you believe to be true about you? What do you think about yourself? Is it positive? Or is it negative? You may tell yourself you are not beautiful, you are not loved, you are not worth it, you are not cared for, but God has never once said that about you. He made you in HIS image, friend. Now it's time to believe that and live out that truth in your life.

Back to 1 Peter 1:13, which says to "prepare your mind for action." This life is a battlefield and you must protect your mind at all costs from the enemy and from the lies of Satan. Whatever is going on in your mind is not truth. So WHAT is truth? Who you are in Christ is truth! When those fleeting negative thoughts come into our minds, we must take hold of those thoughts and not accept them as our own. God wants us to be the best version of ourselves that he created us to be. If you find negative talk going through your mind, this is false and not from God. Those thoughts that are moving you into a better version of yourself - those are from God! Find yourself being more aware of these thoughts and where they come from. Those negative thoughts... push them away.

## THE BATTLE STARTS IN OUR MIND.

And the hardest part of the battle is releasing your negative thoughts and not claiming them as truth. The battle is releasing that of which you THINK defines you, that of which you THINK and believe to be true about you, and releasing that of which you THINK controls you.

So how do you know if something is true? Being in God's word and letting your mind interact with scripture will tell you if it's true or not. In 2 Corinthians 10:5, we read, "We are destroying speculations and every lofty thing raised up against the knowledge of God, and we are taking EVERY THOUGHT CAPTIVE to the obedience of Christ." So are you taking every thought captive? Or are you accepting those thoughts as true? I urge you to take time out each day and throughout your day to pray and focus your thoughts on God. Talk to Him and put Him in your mind so that He will guard it and you will stop believing the lie that you are not worthy and that you cannot do this.

I will leave you with this today,

> "Therefore I urge you, brethren, by the mercies of God, to present your bodies a living and holy sacrifice, acceptable to God, which is your spiritual service of worship." Romans 12:1

As we go through this journey together, my prayer for you is that you would let go of those negative thoughts, stop the negative self talk, and release it all so that you may start believing that your health is worth it. A negative mindset and negative self talk is detrimental in your weight loss journey and can set you back. So take some time today to start creating a new habit and creating new neuro-pathways of thinking. This takes time and requires work, but I can promise you, in the end, it will be worth the journey. So now let's dive in to some tools you can use to change your mindset around your health.

Now take some time with worksheet 2:2 on page 32 and really dive in to your negative thoughts.

Resources:
Amen, D. (2010). Change your brain, change your body. New York: Three Rivers Press.

## MINDFULNESS EXERCISE

Find a quiet space where you can be alone for 5-10 minutes.

Close your eyes and clear your mind of any thoughts and then breathe deeply. Focus only on the physical feelings of breathing—your lungs expanding, air exiting your nostrils, and so on. Other thoughts will pop into your head, but gently bring them back to your breath. Sit here with focus on nothing but your breathing for 5 minutes (set a timer). It will seem hard at first but push through and keep your eyes closed until your timer goes off. Repeat this exercise once a day.

### List Your Goals

I want you to think about why you are doing this (of which we will dive in to shortly!), but for now, I want you to list out your goals below:

<br><br><br><br><br><br><br><br><br>

Now that you have listed your goals, answer the question: were your goals focused on the negative aspect of what you 'don't like about yourself'?

<br><br><br><br><br><br><br>

If you answered YES, then re-write your goals to be in a positive way.

For example don't have your goal be LOSING 10 lbs (that is negative), change that to be, exercising 3x this week (see the positive) or, I am getting all fruits and veggies in each week. The outcome of exercising and eating correctly will be the weight loss. But by changing your outlook on your goals, it will inherently change your mindset around the process. So re-write those goals here:

THINK FIT METHOD *tip*

Put this worksheet up somewhere you can see it daily.

# Negative Thoughts

**Observe your thoughts and write them down.**

Spend 5 minutes monitoring your thoughts about everything: yourself, your job, your life in general etc. It is extremely important to be aware of what negative thoughts are going through your brain. Write them down.

**Write down your triggers.**

Spend 5 more minutes thinking about what triggers you to think these negative things. Write them down. Understanding and bringing into awareness the things that trigger you is very important in changing your thought behavior.

Turn the negative into a positive and make a gratitude list.

Make a list of 10 things you are grateful for and keep it with you all the time. A great place to put this is in your purse or stuck to your computer where you work all day. Every time a negative thought comes into your mind about yourself, take out the paper and speak OUT LOUD the things you are grateful for and what you are celebrating.

1.

2.

3.

4.

5.

6.

7.

8.

9.

10.

Close your eyes and visualize how others see you.

Write down what your friends would say about you or say about your life. Write down what your family would say about you or about your life in general.

Spend some time in prayer asking God to take these negative thoughts captive.
Don't claim these thoughts as your own - give them to God. Write your prayer here:

THINK FIT METHOD *tip*

As you can see, retraining that negative self talk really starts with identifying the
problem and then retraining yourself to speak positive things. By speaking out loud,
your ears are hearing this and you will begin to retrain your brain to think those things
instead of negative things.

# Weekly Reflection

What were the biggest revelations and lessons learned this week?

What are you grateful for this past week?

List three positives of the week when it comes to your nutrition and exercise journey:

List three things you would like to improve on next week.

What concrete actions can you take to work toward these?

When did you take negative thoughts captive this week? List as many as applicable:

From 1-10, how do you feel you did this week?

What does Romans 12:1-2 mean to you this week?

*"Therefore I urge you, brethren, by the mercies of God, to present your bodies
a living and holy sacrifice, acceptable to God, which is your spiritual service
of worship. And do not be conformed to this world, but be transformed by the
renewing of your mind, so that you may prove what the will of God is, that which
is good and acceptable and perfect."*

How can you apply this verse moving forward on this journey?

# WEEK TWO DEVOTIONS

Colossians 3: 1-2

[1] Since, then, you have been raised
with Christ, set your hearts on
things above, where Christ is, seated
at the right hand of God. [2] Set your
minds on things above, not on
earthly things.

The mind is a complex system God gave us and is amazing in the way it works! The mind can also be a trap into a spiral that we will delve into a bit more later with negative self-talk and self-sabotage. There continues to be mass amounts of research done on the brain, what it is, how it works, and how-to re-wire or map the brain. In the book The Power of Habit, Why We Do What We Do in Life and Business, (2012) Charles Duhigg cites a study in which one woman made the conscious decision to stop smoking to attain a goal. By making the decision to stop this one thing and replace it with other healthy options, she changed the brain waves or electrical impulses in her brain. The old behavior impulses were still there however, the healthy ones were over-taking the initial urges to overeat or smoke!

Many times, we look at the mind and think of the brain. Looking at your mind also is about mindfulness. Being conscious and deliberate in our thinking and paying attention to the present allows us to increase our awareness of our own actions. Paul provides us some insights into where to set our minds.

**Read Colossians 3: 1-2**
Take a few minutes to review two things: First, look at your credit card statement or checkbook and see where you spend the bulk of your money. Second, look at your calendar and see where you spend the bulk of your time. Friends this exercise hits me between the eyes every time! Why you might ask? Reviewing where you spend most of your money and your time gives you a glimpse or maybe a whack on the side of your head into where your priorities are.

**Where are your priorities?**
Are there areas you would like to shift? How can you spend more time or money on "things above" versus getting caught up in the day to day hamster wheel?

What can you do to spend quality time with God to set the foundation for your mind?

**Reread Romans 12:2** taking a minute to think about how your mind has transformed as you have walked with God. Utilize your **journal** to capture any of these thoughts.

What areas are you still working on transforming? How are you wanting to transform your health and ultimately your body?

Many times, to transform, we must let go of something. Becoming aware of what we need to let go of is the first step. What are you still hanging onto that may be influencing your mindset? What are some steps you can take to let these items go? Sometimes a ceremony helps as a physical and visual representation of letting go. Maybe the next time you take communion, think of the item being placed in Christ's hands, or write down what you need to let go of and then burn it, or find a beautiful flower to represent what you are letting go of and gently place it in a river or stream, praying over the letting go process. The key then is NOT taking it back or picking it back up again!! Let it go friends and feel freedom with this!

Back to Luke 10:27... "Love the Lord your God with all your heart and with all your soul and with all your strength and with all your mind..."

*Going Deep*

*Allow yourself to take a "nature walk" at least 3 times a week. Do not take anything to eat or drink and do not seek out others. Take your journal and a pen to write down any observations. Choose a threshold and when you step over the threshold, mentally shift your mind to hearing and observing nature. God speaks so many times through the beauty of his creation – so absorb and notice what He is trying to tell you. Don't force where to go but find a place and sit for 15 minutes, closing your eyes if that is easier to start with. Listen with your heart, your mind, and your soul. Note everything and once your "walk" is complete review your notes to see if any messages come to you. Pray before during and after to receive the messages God wants you to bring into your mind! (Horsman, 2015)*

What does it mean to you to love God with all your mind?

What practices do you use today that allow you to focus on Him instead of yourself, the chaos of life, etc.? We need help to ensure we don't allow our thoughts to take us captive. Captive thoughts are those thoughts that control us. Captive thoughts are not given to us by the Holy Spirit, so recognize the captor (Moore, 1999, p. 189)

What do you think is the difference between casual thoughts and captive thoughts?

How can you recognize when you start to move into captive thoughts?

**Read Psalms 26:2. Write** a prayer in your journal asking God to examine your mind and make you aware of when you start to become captive to those thoughts.

In Biblical times, shepherds kept guard over their sheep, vineyards had someone guarding the vines, fortresses had someone on the lookout for persons approaching. These people were called watchmen and friends, my prayer is that you ask God to be your watchman: guarding your mind from negativity, evil and unawareness. Remember Psalms 139:1-2? God knows our thoughts already and where they are headed. Skip to verse 23-24 and humbly ask him to search your heart and your mind. These versus are refreshing as well because God points out that he will be our watchman, because frankly in the battle for our soul, the mind is the battlefield.

## Going Deep

*There are two apps that may help you in this journey to keep your mind on gratitude and help you spend quality time with God listening (and not just talking). The 5 Minute Journal (also available in hard copy) provides a daily quote, has a quick exercise in the morning and one at night helping to focus our minds and review those amazing things that happened during the day. The other app is for meditation and is called Headspace. You can search for topics if you find you are needing some specific guidance or just click on discover to find something new. This app has a free option or a subscription to open more mediations.*

To finish out this section, **Read Proverbs 3:5-6.**

How can you trust the Lord daily with your health journey?

How can you trust him to keep your mind and mindset on that which is healthy?

What outer game plan can you develop so when your mind creeps into negativity you can quickly move out of it?

Resources:
Duhigg, C. (2012). The power of habit: Why we do what we do in life and business. New York: Random House Publishing Group.
Foresight & Strategy. (2015). Dr. John Horsman. Gonzaga University
Moore, B. (1999). Breaking free. Nashville: Adult Ministry Publishing

# Journal it!

_____

_____

_____

_____

_____

_____

_____

_____

_____

_____

_____

_____

_____

_____

_____

_____

_____

_____

_____

_____

_____

If you are in need of a workout plan or nutrition guidance, please jump in to my next virtual bootcamp at jennymire.com or take advantage of the full Think Fit Method portal at thinkfitmethod.com

# **MONDAY** - TRACK YOUR WORKOUT

Exercise: _____

*Rate how you feel*

| Before Workout: | 1 | 2 | 3 | 4 | 5 | 6 | 7 | 8 | 9 | 10 |

| During Workout: | 1 | 2 | 3 | 4 | 5 | 6 | 7 | 8 | 9 | 10 |

| After Workout: | 1 | 2 | 3 | 4 | 5 | 6 | 7 | 8 | 9 | 10 |

Total exercise time: _____    Approximate Calories Burned: _____

Water Goal (oz): _____    Water Consumed (oz): _____

*Today My Win Was:* _____

*Tomorrow I Will:* _____

# **TUESDAY** - TRACK YOUR WORKOUT

Exercise: _____

*Rate how you feel*

| Before Workout: | 1 | 2 | 3 | 4 | 5 | 6 | 7 | 8 | 9 | 10 |

| During Workout: | 1 | 2 | 3 | 4 | 5 | 6 | 7 | 8 | 9 | 10 |

| After Workout: | 1 | 2 | 3 | 4 | 5 | 6 | 7 | 8 | 9 | 10 |

Total exercise time: _____    Approximate Calories Burned: _____

Water Goal (oz): _____    Water Consumed (oz): _____

*Today My Win Was:* _____

*Tomorrow I Will:* _____

# **WEDNESDAY** - TRACK YOUR WORKOUT

Exercise: _____

*Rate how you feel*

| Before Workout: | 1 | 2 | 3 | 4 | 5 | 6 | 7 | 8 | 9 | 10 |
|---|---|---|---|---|---|---|---|---|---|---|

| During Workout: | 1 | 2 | 3 | 4 | 5 | 6 | 7 | 8 | 9 | 10 |
|---|---|---|---|---|---|---|---|---|---|---|

| After Workout: | 1 | 2 | 3 | 4 | 5 | 6 | 7 | 8 | 9 | 10 |
|---|---|---|---|---|---|---|---|---|---|---|

Total exercise time: _____  Approximate Calories Burned: _____

Water Goal (oz): _____  Water Consumed (oz): _____

*Today My Win Was:* _____

*Tomorrow I Will:* _____

# **THURSDAY** - TRACK YOUR WORKOUT

Exercise: _____

*Rate how you feel*

| Before Workout: | 1 | 2 | 3 | 4 | 5 | 6 | 7 | 8 | 9 | 10 |
|---|---|---|---|---|---|---|---|---|---|---|

| During Workout: | 1 | 2 | 3 | 4 | 5 | 6 | 7 | 8 | 9 | 10 |
|---|---|---|---|---|---|---|---|---|---|---|

| After Workout: | 1 | 2 | 3 | 4 | 5 | 6 | 7 | 8 | 9 | 10 |
|---|---|---|---|---|---|---|---|---|---|---|

Total exercise time: _____  Approximate Calories Burned: _____

Water Goal (oz): _____  Water Consumed (oz): _____

*Today My Win Was:* _____

*Tomorrow I Will:* _____

# **FRIDAY** - TRACK YOUR WORKOUT

Exercise: _____

## Rate how you feel

| Before Workout: | 1 | 2 | 3 | 4 | 5 | 6 | 7 | 8 | 9 | 10 |

| During Workout: | 1 | 2 | 3 | 4 | 5 | 6 | 7 | 8 | 9 | 10 |

| After Workout: | 1 | 2 | 3 | 4 | 5 | 6 | 7 | 8 | 9 | 10 |

Total exercise time: _____    Approximate Calories Burned: _____

Water Goal (oz): _____    Water Consumed (oz): _____

Today My Win Was: _____

Tomorrow I Will: _____

# **WEEKEND** - TRACK YOUR WORKOUT

Exercise: _____

## Rate how you feel

| Before Workout: | 1 | 2 | 3 | 4 | 5 | 6 | 7 | 8 | 9 | 10 |

| During Workout: | 1 | 2 | 3 | 4 | 5 | 6 | 7 | 8 | 9 | 10 |

| After Workout: | 1 | 2 | 3 | 4 | 5 | 6 | 7 | 8 | 9 | 10 |

Total exercise time: _____    Approximate Calories Burned: _____

Water Goal (oz): _____    Water Consumed (oz): _____

Today My Win Was: _____

Tomorrow I Will: _____

EMOTIONAL EATING

3

# WEEK
# THREE

# EMOTIONAL EATING

*"All discipline for the moment seems not to be joyful, but sorrowful; yet to those who have been trained by it, afterwards it yields the peaceful fruit of righteousness."*
*Hebrews 12:11*

We've all been there a time or two. Stressed out and overwhelmed to the max, standing over a tub of cookie dough, shoveling spoonfuls into our mouth. Or maybe you find yourself scarfing down french fries and a milkshake, drowning the day's sorrows in a calorie laden binge.

Whether you eat because you are stressed, overwhelmed or depressed, if you find yourself looking to food for comfort, then you are most likely an emotional eater.

## WHAT IS EMOTIONAL EATING?

Emotional eating, or stress eating, is eating to satisfy your emotional needs or to comfort yourself. Typically, emotional eating consists of diving deep into a ton of unhealthy foods that provide little nutritional value, but can bring about a sense of comfort, ease and familiarity.

## SO WHY DO WE EAT EMOTIONALLY?

Most of us engage in emotional eating to cope with negative feelings. We attempt to drown out sorrow in a pint of ice cream, or pan of brownies...similarly to someone who turns to alcohol to ease their troubles. While it isn't a terrible thing to do this on occasion, if turning to food is your main tool for coping with the negative aspects of life, then you are likely to find yourself on a slippery slope that leads to obesity and a whole slew of health issues.

*"I have learned to be content in whatever circumstances I am. I know how to get along with humble means, and I also know how to live in prosperity; in any and every circumstance I have learned the secret of being filled and going hungry, both of having abundance and suffering need. I can do all things through Him who strengthens me."*
*Philippians 4:11-13*

When we don't want to cope with uneasy feelings or emotions, we will turn to comfort food that brings a sense of security. We are turning to food to fill a void in our souls that we don't want to deal with. We turn to "comfort food" to soothe us instead of dealing with the issues head on. Struggling your way through unpleasant feelings can be hard, but it is something that everyone should learn how to do. Philippians 4:11-13 tells us, "I have learned to be content in whatever circumstances I am. I know how to get along with humble means, and I also know how to live in prosperity; in any and every circumstance I have learned the secret of being filled and going hungry, both of having abundance and suffering need. I can do all things through Him who strengthens me." Do you truly believe this? God wants us to learn to be content in everything and that means being content in all the feelings and emotions that may come our way.

Emotional eating can definitely stem from not being content in our feelings, but it's not the only thing that can lead to eating emotionally. A lot of studies out there suggest that people emotionally eat due to a lack of self control. But in my opinion, it is due to other factors. The first one being a true unawareness of what you are doing. Have you ever gotten sad and reached for a bag of chips and before you know it, it is gone? This is being unaware of the feelings that are leading you to eat.

Another reason is that some people tend to only get pleasure from food. Since sugar can release opioids in the brain (just like cocaine and narcotics), it sends your body into a calming or soothing state - just like certain drugs can. So this feeling of getting pleasure from food is real. And it can be very difficult to stop, and in order to do this, we must replace the thing we get pleasure from and find other ways to reward ourselves that feel good.

So how do we stop this? Being mindful of what and when you are eating. Track everything for a while to get a full sense of what you are putting in your body. Try to be overly aware of what you are eating and what state of mind you are in when you are eating it.

We must also learn how to cope with feelings appropriately. Being mad is ok. Being sad is ok. Being happy is ok. Feelings are ok, friends! But working your way through those feelings and sitting in those feelings is better than coping with food.
The first thing in overcoming emotional eating is recognizing if you struggle with it. Head over to page 52 for worksheet 3:1 and complete.

## HUNGER
Now that you've recognized if you struggle with emotional eating or not, let's talk about how to overcome it. The first step to overcoming emotional eating is to recognize it when it's happening.

EMOTIONAL EATING:
- Comes on quickly and seemingly out of nowhere
- Typically will have you craving specific foods
- Comes from your mind, not your stomach
- Isn't satisfying even after you are full

Understanding the difference between emotional hunger and real physical hunger is key.

Emotional hunger comes on suddenly when your anxiety or stress levels begin to rise. Real hunger creeps in slowly, comes from the stomach and is satisfied once you are full. Emotional hunger is a dire need – YOU HAVE TO HAVE IT NOW – whereas physical hunger, again, is gradual.

With emotional eating you lose track of what you're eating and how much you are eating. With physical hunger you are aware of what you are eating.

When you stop emotional eating, you ARE NOT satisfied and you can continue to eat and eat even when you are FULL.

Once you're done with emotional eating you feel GUILTY.

After recognizing when emotional hunger is coming on, you must then determine your triggers and what leads you to want to emotionally eat.

Triggers are what cause you to start eating for any reason other than hunger and nutritional benefit. The best way to avoid emotional eating is to recognize those triggers.

COMMON TRIGGERS CAN INCLUDE:
- Being in social settings (social eating)
- Being overly tired
- Being overly hungry
- Stress
- Being bored
- Drinking alcohol
- Ending every meal with a dessert (ritual)
- Being angry, sad, or overly stressed
- Feeding children and putting meals together quickly

Understanding your triggers will help you better cut off emotional eating before it starts. Some common triggers are stress, sadness, boredom, habit/ritual or a desire to avoid or stuff your emotions. Once you have addressed your trigger(s) - there can be more than one - you will be able to come up with some alternative ways to address the issue.

A great way to start identifying your triggers is to keep a food diary. Write down everything you eat and when you eat it. But not only that, write down what happened in your life prior to eating, how you FELT leading up to eating it and how you felt after eating it. This will help you identify the feelings and triggers that lead to emotional eating.

After identifying your triggers, you must learn to replace the behavior and distract yourself. Instead of turning to food for comfort or relief, try the following:

**When you are stressed or depressed:** go for a run, hit the gym, or do a quick at home workout. The endorphin rush will help you de-stress and you will be doing something good for your body. In addition, you can grab a notepad and start writing. A daily brain dump can significantly reduce stress and help you refocus your mind! If you are really feeling down, call someone you trust and talk things out. If you don't have some-one like that in your life, consider finding a local counselor who could help you walk through your struggles.

**When you are bored:** find something to do other than eat. Workout, read, write, research a topic of interest, call a friend you haven't talked to in a while, clean, or craft. There are countless options for occupying yourself when you are bored. Come up with a list, and keep it posted on your pantry and fridge. This way, every time you want to reach for something to entertain you, you have a host of other options!

**Rituals and Habits:** do you always grab a milkshake on the way home, or some ice cream when you sit down to watch TV every night? Change up your routine. Take a different route home, or make a protein shake at home after work and let that be your new ritual. Instead of ice cream, grab some apples and peanut butter. Same setting, different habit. Habits and rituals are hard to break, so you typically need to replace the behavior while keeping the same outcome.

Emotional eating can be challenging to overcome if you have been doing it for years. It is a powerful and effective way to find relief (temporarily) from life and all the challenges and emotions it brings. In order to stop the emotional eating cycle, you have to make the commitment to find the strength deep within to work on it.

Remember what Hebrews 12:11 says, "All discipline for the moment seems not to be joyful, but sorrowful; yet to those who have been trained by it, afterwards it yields the peaceful fruit of righteousness." It is hard in the moment friends, but the discipline of saying no and putting down that spoon yields great return!

One of my most favorite passages is Romans 5:3-4.

*"And not only this, but we also exult in our tribulations, knowing that tribulation brings about perseverance; and perseverance, proven character; and proven character, hope; and hope does not disappoint, because the love of God has been poured out within our hearts through the Holy Spirit who was given to us."*

I want you to know that today, whatever you may be struggling with that causes you stress, grief, sadness, pain - anything at all - that God has you in His hand. That these tribulations will bring out so much hope. Let's address this emotional eating and start changing the behavior - head over to page 53 for worksheet 3:2 and complete.

# Emotional Eating

Do you continually reward yourself with food?

Do you eat more when you feel stressed?

Do you eat when you are not hungry only to feel better or self soothe?

Do you feel out of control around food or feel that food controls you?

Do you have food FOMO (Fear of Missing Out)?
If you see someone eating a cookie or trying the latest Starbucks drink that is packed with sugar, do you HAVE to have it so you don't "miss out?"

Do you have extreme guilt after you eat something you know you shouldn't have?

If you answered yes to any of these questions, you most likely struggle with emotional eating to some degree or another. But don't be alarmed, more people than you struggle with this, so you are not alone!

# Addresing Emotional Eating
## +
# Re-writing Your Rituals

What's going on in your life right now (trials and tribulations) that's making you want to eat?

What emotion(s) are you experiencing? (sad, mad, etc)

Will eating right now make you feel better? If so, for how long will you feel better?

If you choose to eat, will it create any NEW problems or lead to guilt?

What daily ritual do you fall into that causes you to eat when you shouldn't? (driving by fast food, having a snack when I get home, etc)

List out 5 things you can do to destress yourself (DO NOT LIST EAT!).

1.

2.

3.

4.

5.

List out 5 things you can do when you are bored. (DO NOT LIST EAT!).

1.

2.

3.

4.

5.

What are some healthy food options you can turn to when you feel a trigger coming on? (ie: fruit, veggies, air popped popcorn, gum, sparkling water)

What are some non food options you can turn to when you feel a trigger coming on? (ie: wash hands, put on chapstick, brush teeth, call a friend, cleaning, journaling)

THINK FIT METHOD *tip*

Repeat the first and second questions on this page as many times as needed.

# Weekly Reflection

What were the biggest revelations and lessons learned this week?

What are you grateful for this past week?

List three positives of the week when it comes to your nutrition and exercise journey:

List three things you would like to improve on next week.

What concrete actions can you take to work toward these?

When did you stop yourself from emotional eating? List as many as applicable:

From 1-10, how do you feel you did this week?

What does Hebrews 12:11 mean to you this week?
*"All discipline for the moment seems not to be joyful, but sorrowful; yet to those who have been trained by it, afterwards it yields the peaceful fruit of righteousness."*

How can you apply this verse moving forward on this journey?

# WEEK THREE DEVOTIONS

2 Timothy 1:7

[7] For the Spirit God gave
us does not make us timid,
but gives us power, love and self-
discipline.

*W*hat are emotions and why do we even have to deal with them?

"Emotions are physical sensations combined with thoughts and beliefs about particular events and people." (Christian Bible Studies, Introduction)

Sometimes we confuse emotions to the physical sensation alone or there is an emotion attached we may or may not be consciously aware of. For instance, the physical sensation of hunger may arise because our bodies need fed where as other times (and friends I find this to be the case with me numerous times) the sensation occurs because it is the way to numb an emotion. When we get into this state we need to pull from the previous study and be aware.... be very aware and mindful of what our emotions and our bodies are telling us. Williamson, (2012) shares that it is important to know how you can and sometime how you cannot process emotions.

## Digging Deeper

*Be aware of each emotion and how your process through. Make a list of those emotions and more – anger, frustration, joy, sorrow, shame, pride, heartbreak, etc. Once you made list, make statements such as – I am angry at _____ then fill in the blank. Ensure you take the time to write it out! Get it out of your mind, heart and soul which then removes it from your body! Once you have written about the emotion, Pray surrendering your emotion, in this case anger and asking God to take it away from you. (Williamson, 2012, p. 30-39) Utilize your journal and note any awareness that comes to you.*

In this Think Fit Method journal, numerous reasons why someone might take part in emotional eating is mentioned. For the sake of this study we will be focusing on facing the emotions we are wanting to bolt, numb or cover up! Roth, (2011, p. 40-41) that when we eat to avoid or numb emotions we are actually living in reverse. You see it's the pain which has already happened that we are avoiding – not the present moment. When you realize this and combat it with God's spirit of power you actually feel more alive because you are living in the moment and actually feeling!!

**Read 2 Timothy 1:7**: You see, God gives us his Holy Spirit and the spirit is powerful! Paul also talks about how this spirit is of love and self-discipline.

How does knowing God's Holy Spirit is in you give you confidence to face whatever past emotions have been stuck in your body, mind and spirit?

How does knowing God provides an unearthly way of loving yourself and others give you assurance as you progress in this health journey?

"Emotions must be acknowledged and felt; or else they cannot be learned from, grown from, or processed" (Williamson, 2010, p 171).

**Special Note:** Some of us may need to seek out a professional to discuss our emotions at a deeper level, creating both inner and outer game plans that are healthy for our body, mind, soul and heart. Seeking out a credentialed counselor who shares your faith base can be very beneficial!

As you continue to shift your perspectives in this health journey, you need to have support. Friends, I don't just mean a workout partner but rather people in your life who you feel you can be vulnerable and authentic with. Go back to your list of 5 people. Do any of these folks allow you to process emotions in a safe and vulnerable state? If so, that is fantastic!! If you don't have a few close people whom you feel you can do this with, try to identify some and have a conversation with them about being a cloud of witnesses to you, helping you to process as emotional triggers occur so you may run the race set before you!

### Digging Deeper

Go back to week 1, worksheet 2 on page 12, to review your motivation – the answer to the why question. Now using this same 5 Why Technique, ask yourself why you want to eat? Once you answer the first why, keep going... the more you practice this technique the more aware you will become of the patterns that need to be shifted. Awareness is a powerful tool and can lead you to uncover more and more about the emotions you are not wanting to face and turning to food for. This journal provides a great list of outer game plans that can aid you as you face these emotions...make good use of these! Take some time to meditate and pray on the why's, utilize your journal and jot down any awareness that comes to you on this topic. Practice this technique every time you start to eat and you will notice changes in your mindset about why you are eating will begin to occur.

**Read Hebrews 12:1-2.** "Let us fix our eyes on Jesus..." take my thoughts to another time when Jesus asked Peter to fix his eyes on Him and not the waves.

**Read Matthew 14: 22-33.** What about this story is relevant to you and the storms that go on in your mind?

Gods spirit in us and our minds become the master versus the slave of our inner storms. "Your task, therefore, is to give your feelings to God, that you might be lifted above the storms of your subconscious mind. The storms are raging for one reason only: your inner self will not be ignored" (Williamson, 2010, p. 172-173). Build your spiritual mastery so you can release the bonds of emotional slavery! Only by surrendering your self-will can you gain spiritual mastery. Just think, by giving these emotions to God, you are giving it to The Almighty to handle....remember Romans 8:31 "If God is for us, who can be against us"...

**Journal** your thoughts from this lesson. Take time to **meditate, pray and ponder** on your thoughts and the emotions that arise from these exercises!

References:
Christianity Today International. (2011). Study through the bible Psalms: Managing our emotions [Ebook]. Retrieved from http://ChristianBibleStudies.com
Roth, G. (2011). Women, food and God. New York: Scribner.
Williamson, M. (2012). A course in weight loss. Carlsbad, Calif.: Hay House.

*Journal it!*

If you are in need of a workout plan or nutrition guidance, please jump in to my next virtual bootcamp at jennymire.com or take advantage of the full Think Fit Method portal at thinkfitmethod.com

# **MONDAY** - TRACK YOUR WORKOUT

Exercise: _____

*Rate how you feel*

| Before Workout: | 1 | 2 | 3 | 4 | 5 | 6 | 7 | 8 | 9 | 10 |
|---|---|---|---|---|---|---|---|---|---|---|

| During Workout: | 1 | 2 | 3 | 4 | 5 | 6 | 7 | 8 | 9 | 10 |
|---|---|---|---|---|---|---|---|---|---|---|

| After Workout: | 1 | 2 | 3 | 4 | 5 | 6 | 7 | 8 | 9 | 10 |
|---|---|---|---|---|---|---|---|---|---|---|

Total exercise time: _____     Approximate Calories Burned: _____

Water Goal (oz): _____     Water Consumed (oz): _____

*Today My Win Was:* _____

*Tomorrow I Will:* _____

# **TUESDAY** - TRACK YOUR WORKOUT

Exercise: _____

*Rate how you feel*

| Before Workout: | 1 | 2 | 3 | 4 | 5 | 6 | 7 | 8 | 9 | 10 |
|---|---|---|---|---|---|---|---|---|---|---|

| During Workout: | 1 | 2 | 3 | 4 | 5 | 6 | 7 | 8 | 9 | 10 |
|---|---|---|---|---|---|---|---|---|---|---|

| After Workout: | 1 | 2 | 3 | 4 | 5 | 6 | 7 | 8 | 9 | 10 |
|---|---|---|---|---|---|---|---|---|---|---|

Total exercise time: _____     Approximate Calories Burned: _____

Water Goal (oz): _____     Water Consumed (oz): _____

*Today My Win Was:* _____

*Tomorrow I Will:* _____

# **WEDNESDAY** - TRACK YOUR WORKOUT

Exercise: _____

*Rate how you feel*

| Before Workout: | 1 | 2 | 3 | 4 | 5 | 6 | 7 | 8 | 9 | 10 |
|---|---|---|---|---|---|---|---|---|---|---|

| During Workout: | 1 | 2 | 3 | 4 | 5 | 6 | 7 | 8 | 9 | 10 |
|---|---|---|---|---|---|---|---|---|---|---|

| After Workout: | 1 | 2 | 3 | 4 | 5 | 6 | 7 | 8 | 9 | 10 |
|---|---|---|---|---|---|---|---|---|---|---|

Total exercise time: _____    Approximate Calories Burned: _____

Water Goal (oz): _____    Water Consumed (oz): _____

*Today My Win Was:* _____

*Tomorrow I Will:* _____

# **THURSDAY** - TRACK YOUR WORKOUT

Exercise: _____

*Rate how you feel*

| Before Workout: | 1 | 2 | 3 | 4 | 5 | 6 | 7 | 8 | 9 | 10 |
|---|---|---|---|---|---|---|---|---|---|---|

| During Workout: | 1 | 2 | 3 | 4 | 5 | 6 | 7 | 8 | 9 | 10 |
|---|---|---|---|---|---|---|---|---|---|---|

| After Workout: | 1 | 2 | 3 | 4 | 5 | 6 | 7 | 8 | 9 | 10 |
|---|---|---|---|---|---|---|---|---|---|---|

Total exercise time: _____    Approximate Calories Burned: _____

Water Goal (oz): _____    Water Consumed (oz): _____

*Today My Win Was:* _____

*Tomorrow I Will:* _____

# **FRIDAY** - TRACK YOUR WORKOUT

Exercise: _____

## Rate how you feel

| Before Workout: | 1 | 2 | 3 | 4 | 5 | 6 | 7 | 8 | 9 | 10 |

| During Workout: | 1 | 2 | 3 | 4 | 5 | 6 | 7 | 8 | 9 | 10 |

| After Workout: | 1 | 2 | 3 | 4 | 5 | 6 | 7 | 8 | 9 | 10 |

Total exercise time: _____    Approximate Calories Burned: _____

Water Goal (oz): _____    Water Consumed (oz): _____

Today My Win Was: _____

Tomorrow I Will: _____

# **WEEKEND** - TRACK YOUR WORKOUT

Exercise: _____

## Rate how you feel

| Before Workout: | 1 | 2 | 3 | 4 | 5 | 6 | 7 | 8 | 9 | 10 |

| During Workout: | 1 | 2 | 3 | 4 | 5 | 6 | 7 | 8 | 9 | 10 |

| After Workout: | 1 | 2 | 3 | 4 | 5 | 6 | 7 | 8 | 9 | 10 |

Total exercise time: _____    Approximate Calories Burned: _____

Water Goal (oz): _____    Water Consumed (oz): _____

Today My Win Was: _____

Tomorrow I Will: _____

SELF SABOTAGE

4

# WEEK
# FOUR

*"Like a city that is broken into and without walls is a man who has no control over his spirit." Proverbs 25:28*

I want to start off by asking you a question.

## *DO YOU WANT TO BE MORE THAN YOU EVER THOUGHT YOU COULD BE?*

Really ask yourself that. Do you want to be MORE than what you ever thought you could be?

# SELF SABOTAGE

This is a topic that is dear to my heart because of my background in mental health and social work... and because I continue to struggle with this day in and day out. Yep, even I struggle with this.

*"Watch over your heart with all diligence, for from it flow the springs of life."*

*Proverbs 4:23*

According to *Psychology Today* , "Behavior is said to be self-sabotaging when it creates problems and interferes with long-standing goals. The most common self-sabotaging behaviors are procrastination, self-medication with drugs or alcohol, and comfort eating. These acts may seem helpful in the moment, but they ultimately undermine us, especially when we engage in them repeatedly."

This definition alone hits home in a hard way! How many of us sabotage ourselves from reaching a goal? I know I do!

When we self sabotage, it feels like we've hit an invisible brick wall that we don't recognize until we feel the pain. Typically we are not aware we are self sabotaging until we feel like a failure.

Is this true to you?

This week, we are bringing that self sabotaging behavior, that brick wall, into awareness. We are going to practice seeing it for what it is and ACKNOWLEDGE it - even though it's hard. And it's ok that it's hard. We will be working on creating new neuro-pathways by creating a new consistent routine, and that is HARD work. But once you acknowledge your brick wall, you then have the choice to do something about it.

There are so many ways one can self sabotage, but for the sake of Think Fit Method, we are going to talk about the eating and exercising side of self sabotage.

I want to offer you a great example of self sabotage. It goes like this:

*You are eating great all day, nutrition is on point and you're getting the nutrients your body needs. You feel good. Until your coworker brings in cupcakes and says those dreaded words: "Just have one. It won't kill you!" So you start to rationalize it in your head telling yourself, "Well, I did get my workout in today, and it will only be one" – and before you know it, you have devoured the cupcake in less than 5 seconds. After that, some guilt sets in and you get mad at yourself. A few minutes later you are looking at those cupcakes telling yourself that you already blew it for the day so why not eat another... and then that second leads to a third and fourth. By the time you get home from work, you think you've already messed up so bad so why not order pizza for dinner.*

Basically, instead of just stopping at that one cupcake, you have sabotaged the whole day.

But it also can happen with your workouts.

Missing one workout is not the same as missing five workouts. Or that day you think to yourself, "I only have 30 minutes today," there is no possible way to get in my full good workout, so I just won't do it.

The thing is, a 30 minute workout is better than no workout. So it's the same concept as the food – our minds play tricks on us and our subconscious will start talking us out of working out all together. Your mind is a POWERFUL thing friend. Be aware of this!

Self sabotaging behavior is never worth it! Think about it! Have you ever felt good afterwards? Has there ever been a positive out of it? No. Typically you feel like a failure, right?

So why do we self sabotage? Well, there are many different reasons. The first being stress. When we are about to embark on something new or something unfamiliar, our brain says STOP! Our subconscious goes in to a state of survival and we want to go back to the familiar. We want to stay safe and fight against the unfamiliar territory. This is why it is so common to struggle with self sabotage when we are making lifestyle changes with our health and wellness. It's new. It's unfamiliar. It's hard. So our subconscious will push us back into the SAFE and FAMILIAR territory of comfort food etc. When that happens, the negative self talk sets in saying, "I'm a failure," "I can't do this," "why even try," "I can't stop eating this way." And when you fight against this old brain and subconscious, it will fight back harder making it difficult to change.

**The first step** is to examine and identify your triggers. There are two types of triggers:

*I WANT TO GIVE YOU A FEW STEPS YOU CAN TAKE TO STOP THOSE BEHAVIORS WHEN IT COMES TO YOUR HEALTH GOALS.*

Emotional and Environmental/Physical.

So what sets you off to where you think you just don't care anymore? Is it when you're stressed (emotional)? If so, what are you stressed about? Continue to ask yourself questions until you dig deep to the root of the trigger. It may be that one coworker who continually brings in treats to the office (environmental trigger). Or it may be when you are feeling overwhelmed with work and home life (emotional trigger). Whatever it is, you must identify the trigger.

Head over to worksheet 4:1 on page 70 to work on identifying your trigger.

Now that you have identified your triggers, you will need to continually tell yourself **YOU CAN STOP AT ONE**. I get this... it is HARD to stop at just one treat once you've started. This is a personal struggle of my own that I deal with all the time. But the more you say it out loud to yourself, the easier it becomes to believe it and follow through with it. It's true, one small treat here and there is ok and it will NOT ruin your whole day or week. It is easy to bounce back from. But if you let that guilt get the best of you, it will drag you down and the self sabotaging begins!

Triggers produce unwanted impulses. And those unwanted impulses are seeking something.... either fulfillment or acknowledgement. Impulses are not something you should fight against, but instead you should learn to acknowledge these triggers instead of fulfilling them.

Next, we need to desensitize ourselves to our triggers by having a plan in place. Sometimes the plan will need to be as drastic as not even having a taste of that treat. But other times having a small taste is all you need to push past the self sabotage and to desensitize yourself to that trigger of being around tempting food.

In the process of beating those self sabotaging behaviors, you must also be cognizant of the immediate outcome.

If you resist that cupcake in the workplace today, will you feel better today? **ABSOLUTELY.**

If you get that 10 minute workout in, will you immediately be proud of yourself? YES! So continue to tell yourself, "If I workout today, I will feel better TODAY" and "If I stop at one cookie, I will be proud TODAY that I had the willpower to stop at one." It is imperative to recognize the immediate outcome and not always have your eyes on the long term goal.

Understanding your triggers and putting an action plan in place are tough things, but we are here today to work on ourselves, right? You made the commitment to YOU, so let's get to work. Move on to worksheet 4:2 and complete.

Every time you overcome those triggers, you are creating new neuro-pathways in your brain which in turn eventually create new habits and new rituals. Once these neuro-pathways are set, you no longer have the desire to stay in the old because you have created a new normal and you have shown yourself you are SAFE in this new normal. This is a huge step to overcoming self sabotage behaviors. And every time you overcome those triggers, I want you to CELEBRATE. Celebrate that victory and focus on it. Those are the wins worth celebrating and recognizing day in and day out.

*"Set a guard, O Lord, over my mouth; Keep watch over the door of my lips. Do not incline my heart to any evil thing, to practice deeds of wickedness with men who do iniquity: and do not let me eat of their delicacies." Psalms 141: 3-4*

Resources
Psychology Today: Health, Help, Happiness + Find a Therapist. (2018). Retrieved from https://www.psychologytoday.com/us

# Know Your Triggers + Be Aware of Your Brick Walls

## EXAMPLES OF EMOTIONAL & ENVIRONMENTAL TRIGGERS:

- Being alone
- Being lonely
- Being bored
- Feeling depressed
- Feeling sick
- Celebrating
- Being excited
- Being overly hungry
- Feeling frustrated
- Being in a large group of people
- Being at work
- Being in a car
- Driving by restaurants
- Cooking for yourself
- Cooking for your kids
- Being at a social event
- Being at a party
- Feeling unworthy or rejected
- Being near tempting foods
- Feeling grumpy
- Being tired
- Feeling anxious
- Being in certain areas of your house
- Certain times of day
- Being over scheduled (going non stop)
- Being around certain people
- Feeling overwhelmed
- Feeling chaotic
- When others are "trying" out the tempting food

When do you feel the most "out of control" when it comes to your health and wellness?

Finish this sentence:
"I am at higher risk of sabotaging my health and wellness goals when..."

What is it about these emotions or happenings that make them become an issue for you?
Maybe you feel impulsive during these times? Or irrational? Or just not sure what to do? Or are you just looking for comfort? Or is it because it is what you know and you feel comfortable making these choices?

Do you feel that any of these triggers bring up a memory or an emotional state that you don't want to deal with and so you turn to comfort? If so, what emotion or memory?

Now that you have identified some potential triggers, we need to address what to do with them and how to have a plan in place for the next time you recognize it is happening. Head back to the education section of week 4 on page 66 and continue on.

# Self Sabotage Action Plan

When I start to recognize my triggers and I want to eat, I am going to: (ie: call a friend, drink some water etc...)

When I start to recognize my triggers and I want to skip my workout, I am going to:

List 3-5 healthy snack options:

Now that you've listed some healthy options, make yourself a little "trigger survival kit" with these snack foods, including a bottle of water.

Place one of these in your workplace, in your car, and in your kitchen. When you feel the need to make poor food choices based on your triggers, pull out this Trigger Survival Kit and choose a healthy snack.

THINK FIT METHOD  *tip*

Some tips for when you recognize your triggers coming on and you start to feel your excuses coming up:

1. Acknowledge that trigger and bring awareness to it in your mind.

2. Breathe in and out slowly for 2 minutes closing your eyes and focusing solely on your breathing in your mind's eye.

3. In your mind's eye, shine the light on your immediate reward for not letting that trigger win. Focus on the victory, not the negative.

4. Talk to someone about it or journal about it.

# Weekly Reflection

What were the biggest revelations and lessons learned this week?

What are you grateful for this past week?

List three positives of the week when it comes to your nutrition and exercise journey:

1.

2.

3.

List three things you would like to improve on next week.
What concrete actions can you take to work towards these?

When did you recognize triggers and the onset of self sabotage behavior? List as many as applicable:

From 1-10, how do you feel you did this week?

What does Proverbs 25:28 mean to you this week?

"Like a city that is broken into and without walls is a man who has no control over his spirit."
Proverbs 25:28

How can you apply this verse moving forward on this journey?

# WEEK FOUR DEVOTIONS

## 1 John 1:5-10

[5] This is the message we have heard from him and declare to you: God is light; in him there is no darkness at all. [6] If we claim to have fellowship with him and yet walk in the darkness, we lie and do not live out the truth. [7] But if we walk in the light, as he is in the light, we have fellowship with one another, and the blood of Jesus, his Son, purifies us from all[a] sin.

[8] If we claim to be without sin, we deceive ourselves and the truth is not in us. [9] If we confess our sins, he is faithful and just and will forgive us our sins and purify us from all unrighteousness. [10] If we claim we have not sinned, we make him out to be a liar and his word is not in us.

*W*e are not made to be perfect, but rather imperfect. This also relates to our health and fitness journey!

**Read I John 1:5-10.** John explains starting in verse 8 how we mess up all the time...so friends its better to accept this and be prepared for when it does happen! Make sure you have completed worksheet 4:1 and 4:2 before moving on!

How does it help to know you will self-sabotage? I know for me it has allowed me to have more grace for myself which then stops me from eating the next cupcake and ordering the pizza when I get home!

How does it help you to know you have a plan in place to help combat this?

Take a few minutes and **journal** not what you will do, but rather how you will feel when you do sabotage and you actually stop yourself from going to far down that path. Again, make sure to focus on feelings.

How can you turn to Christ when you feel your triggers or eat that one cupcake and start beating yourself up?

Let's move over to Hebrews to see what Paul says about temptation...**Read Hebrew 4:15-16.** Now don't get me wrong, I'm not suggesting eating a cupcake is a sin. Sin really is anything that gets in the way of our relationship with God...I don't know about you, but there have been plenty of times the emotions such as guilt and shame associated with my food choices and how I beat myself up after jumping into the cycle of eating have come in the way of my relationship with Christ. Paul is reminding us that we are not alone...Christ has also been tempted in many ways and understands what we are going through! **Read 1 Corinthians 10: 12-13** spending a few minutes meditating on this scripture.

How does knowing God will provide a way out provide you confidence in facing your triggers?

Even though we may plan an outer game strategy, there will be times we run or bolt from our well laid plans. Bolting is a desire to numb, avoid or leave that which we face. Sometimes we are not even aware we are bolting from something. Take a few minutes to look at your patterns. **Utilize your journal** and identify not only when you bolt, but what you are feeling when you bolt. **Pray**, asking God to remove these feelings and temptations from you, realizing more than likely will come up again and again.

**Read Romans 7:15-25.** When you feel those triggers coming or maybe you weren't even aware but are right in the middle of it...stop, breathe and pray my friends! There are so many times I've used this technique to bring me back into a state of awareness versus letting my critter brain take over.

## Digging Deeper

*Figuring out how our conscious and subconscious brains process our desire to bolt sometimes takes a deeper exercise. Looking at and listening to our "thin self" and "not so thin self" can provide some helpful insights. Take some time on this exercise and try to be as honest and transparent as possible. This is an exercise to show love, grace and compassion, but also to get those not so great feelings out, sharing with both sides of yourself because each wants to be heard. Ask God to guide you in this process and write a letter to the not so thin you from the thin you, expressing your feelings and thoughts. Then allow the not so thin you to respond back (write another letter from the not so thin you to the thin you). Journal any insights you gained in this exercise, praying for continued guidance. (Williamson, 2012, p 48-52)*

*Resources*
*Williamson, M. (2012). A course in weight loss. Carlsbad, Calif.: Hay House.*

## Journal it!

If you are in need of a workout plan or nutrition guidance, please jump in to my next virtual bootcamp at jennymire.com or take advantage of the full Think Fit Method portal at thinkfitmethod.com

# **MONDAY** - TRACK YOUR WORKOUT

Exercise: _____

## *Rate how you feel*

| Before Workout: | 1 | 2 | 3 | 4 | 5 | 6 | 7 | 8 | 9 | 10 |
|---|---|---|---|---|---|---|---|---|---|---|

| During Workout: | 1 | 2 | 3 | 4 | 5 | 6 | 7 | 8 | 9 | 10 |
|---|---|---|---|---|---|---|---|---|---|---|

| After Workout: | 1 | 2 | 3 | 4 | 5 | 6 | 7 | 8 | 9 | 10 |
|---|---|---|---|---|---|---|---|---|---|---|

Total exercise time: _____     Approximate Calories Burned: _____

Water Goal (oz): _____     Water Consumed (oz): _____

*Today My Win Was:* _____

*Tomorrow I Will:* _____

# **TUESDAY** - TRACK YOUR WORKOUT

Exercise: _____

## *Rate how you feel*

| Before Workout: | 1 | 2 | 3 | 4 | 5 | 6 | 7 | 8 | 9 | 10 |
|---|---|---|---|---|---|---|---|---|---|---|

| During Workout: | 1 | 2 | 3 | 4 | 5 | 6 | 7 | 8 | 9 | 10 |
|---|---|---|---|---|---|---|---|---|---|---|

| After Workout: | 1 | 2 | 3 | 4 | 5 | 6 | 7 | 8 | 9 | 10 |
|---|---|---|---|---|---|---|---|---|---|---|

Total exercise time: _____     Approximate Calories Burned: _____

Water Goal (oz): _____     Water Consumed (oz): _____

*Today My Win Was:* _____

*Tomorrow I Will:* _____

# **WEDNESDAY** - TRACK YOUR WORKOUT

Exercise: _____

*Rate how you feel*

| Before Workout: | 1 | 2 | 3 | 4 | 5 | 6 | 7 | 8 | 9 | 10 |
|---|---|---|---|---|---|---|---|---|---|---|

| During Workout: | 1 | 2 | 3 | 4 | 5 | 6 | 7 | 8 | 9 | 10 |
|---|---|---|---|---|---|---|---|---|---|---|

| After Workout: | 1 | 2 | 3 | 4 | 5 | 6 | 7 | 8 | 9 | 10 |
|---|---|---|---|---|---|---|---|---|---|---|

Total exercise time: _____    Approximate Calories Burned: _____

Water Goal (oz): _____    Water Consumed (oz): _____

*Today My Win Was:* _____

*Tomorrow I Will:* _____

# **THURSDAY** - TRACK YOUR WORKOUT

Exercise: _____

*Rate how you feel*

| Before Workout: | 1 | 2 | 3 | 4 | 5 | 6 | 7 | 8 | 9 | 10 |
|---|---|---|---|---|---|---|---|---|---|---|

| During Workout: | 1 | 2 | 3 | 4 | 5 | 6 | 7 | 8 | 9 | 10 |
|---|---|---|---|---|---|---|---|---|---|---|

| After Workout: | 1 | 2 | 3 | 4 | 5 | 6 | 7 | 8 | 9 | 10 |
|---|---|---|---|---|---|---|---|---|---|---|

Total exercise time: _____    Approximate Calories Burned: _____

Water Goal (oz): _____    Water Consumed (oz): _____

*Today My Win Was:* _____

*Tomorrow I Will:* _____

# **FRIDAY** - TRACK YOUR WORKOUT

Exercise: _____

*Rate how you feel*

| Before Workout: | 1 | 2 | 3 | 4 | 5 | 6 | 7 | 8 | 9 | 10 |
|---|---|---|---|---|---|---|---|---|---|---|

| During Workout: | 1 | 2 | 3 | 4 | 5 | 6 | 7 | 8 | 9 | 10 |
|---|---|---|---|---|---|---|---|---|---|---|

| After Workout: | 1 | 2 | 3 | 4 | 5 | 6 | 7 | 8 | 9 | 10 |
|---|---|---|---|---|---|---|---|---|---|---|

Total exercise time: _____     Approximate Calories Burned: _____

Water Goal (oz): _____     Water Consumed (oz): _____

*Today My Win Was:* _____

*Tomorrow I Will:* _____

# **WEEKEND** - TRACK YOUR WORKOUT

Exercise: _____

*Rate how you feel*

| Before Workout: | 1 | 2 | 3 | 4 | 5 | 6 | 7 | 8 | 9 | 10 |
|---|---|---|---|---|---|---|---|---|---|---|

| During Workout: | 1 | 2 | 3 | 4 | 5 | 6 | 7 | 8 | 9 | 10 |
|---|---|---|---|---|---|---|---|---|---|---|

| After Workout: | 1 | 2 | 3 | 4 | 5 | 6 | 7 | 8 | 9 | 10 |
|---|---|---|---|---|---|---|---|---|---|---|

Total exercise time: _____     Approximate Calories Burned: _____

Water Goal (oz): _____     Water Consumed (oz): _____

*Today My Win Was:* _____

*Tomorrow I Will:* _____

NEGATIVE SELF TALK

5

# WEEK
# FIVE

# NEGATIVE SELF-TALK

*"Finally, brethren, whatever is true, whatever is honorable, whatever is right, whatever is pure, whatever is lovely, whatever is of good repute, if there is any excellence and if anything worthy of praise, dwell on these things." Philippians 4:8*

*N*egative Self Talk. Who does it? Me, me, me! I'm raising my hand with you!

WE ALL STRUGGLE WITH NEGATIVE SELF TALK TO ONE DEGREE OR ANOTHER.

Language is a powerful thing, and it's not just the words we say out loud - it is the words and comments that run through our brain.

Back in week 2 we addressed Mindset and discussed how the mind body connection works, but this week I really want to dig deep into negative self talk.

HAVE YOU EVER SAT AND REALLY MONITORED YOUR THOUGHTS ABOUT YOURSELF?

Most of us haven't but I challenge you today to do that. Take 5 minutes RIGHT NOW and really think about the thoughts you have about yourself. Remember in week 2, we talked about "Cognitive Behavioral Therapy" and how it is influenced by the belief that thoughts influence feelings, which then influence behavior. You start to behave and feel as if those negative thoughts are true. By having a constant negative feeling towards yourself it will manifest in every aspect of your life.

But why is this detrimental? A 2013 study by Florida State University College of Medicine found that teens who were considered normal weight but had negative thoughts about their weight were more likely to end up obese later in life.

*God calls to take every thought captive. Negative thoughts about outselves are not of God. When those negative thougth come in, give it to God!*

Words carry energy, just like anything else, and that energy is a very powerful thing. And having this negative energy in your body can lead to stress and depressive tendencies, which slows the metabolism. This negative energy can also lead you to overeating (emotional eating) to numb the feeling, of which we addressed in week 3. So not only are you sabotaging your health by slowing the metabolism, but you are creating a cycle of negative self talk over and over again. Negative self talk can also lead to physical and emotional stress that can harm your cardiovascular health, gut health, and immune system by slowing the metabolism and making weight loss virtually impossible.

> *"We are destroying speculations and every lofty thing raised up against the knowledge of God, and we are taking every thought captive to the obedience of Christ."*
> *2 Corinthians 10:5*

> *"When my anxious thoughts multiply within me, your consolations delight my souls." Psalms 94:19*

Now we are going to work hard on overcoming negative self talk and giving it back to God. Head over to worksheet 5:1 on page 90 and complete.

## GUT HEALTH

Now that we have realized how detrimental negative self talk can be to our overall health, let's talk about gut health and why it is so important.

> *"It is not good to eat too much honey, nor is it glory to search out one's own glory."*
> *Proverbs 25:27*

It is so important to have healthy gut bacteria, yet it's something that is just now coming to the forefront of the industry.

Doctors typically recommend probiotics to increase the good bacteria in your digestive system, since they will help naturally break down food. This is especially important when your digestive system is compromised (such as having no gallbladder - like myself).

Research shows that having the wrong bacteria in our gut may cause unhealthy cravings by controlling our hormones that connect our brain to our gut. Bad gut bacteria opens up a world of chaos for our bodies— a vast array of health issues stem as a result of this. Let's start off by addressing the weight loss issue and how it corresponds to gut health. The bacteria you have in your gut may go hand in hand with your ability or inability to lose weight. Having an overload of the wrong bacteria can cause massive cravings and stop our ability to convert some food molecules into short chain fatty acids - which in turn control our ability to prevent fat storage and use fat stores as energy.

But not only does bad bacteria in our gut cause us to hold on to unwanted fat, or cause cravings, it may also be the cause of so much more. Scientists are discovering that your gut health impacts so much more than just your digestion - it can impact your entire body and mental state.

Let's talk about just a few other things it can impact: autoimmune conditions, allergy problems, emotional distress (anxiety, low self control regarding food choices) and more. Do you see your struggles regarding health and wellness in any of these? Most of us can. This is why gut health is paramount in our overall health and why I teach my clients how to integrate a nutrition protocol that will address this from a food standpoint but also something that can help even from day one: Probiotics.

The right probiotic actually supports a healthy fat metabolism. The ability to control fat metabolism is huge, ladies! Weight loss, or even maintaining weight, is not as easy or as simple as calories in vs. calories out.

According to Dr. Kiran Krishnan, a microbiologist, the science behind the right probiotic states that "the spores have the highly valuable ability to convert starches and nonstarch polysaccharides from the diet into short-chain fatty acids (SCFAs). These SCFAs control fat burn, prevention of fat storage, energy harvesting from food, gastric emptying, insulin sensitivity, satiety, and a whole host of other metabolic parameters. When increased, they essentially reprogram your body to burn more fat and store less fat."

## PROBIOTICS

Not all probiotics need to be refrigerated- according to Dr. Krishnan, it depends on the type. But it used to be commonly understood that 'living bacteria' was the 'best.' Research has come a long way, and we now know there are certain strains, like the bacillus, that can survive the stomach and make it all the way to the intestines where they are needed most.

Yogurt really doesn't give you what you need when it comes to probiotics. "For starters, look at the nutritional value of many yogurts and compare them to the supposed benefits. Yogurt is often filled with sugar (sometimes even more than a chocolate bar), which in itself can actually kill the beneficial bacteria in your gut."

All good bacteria does not mean they are acting as a true probiotic. There are trillions of bacteria in your intestinal tract, and we are still identifying and understanding their role in the human body. Many of these bacteria have been identified as "good," but not all of them are the same. A true probiotic is one that can help colonize the body with helpful bacteria.

This truly is an amazing thing! For more information on how you can get some probiotics for yourself, check them out at jennymirefitness.com/supplements

Some common signs that you have poor gut health include digestive issues such as constipation, bloating, gas or diarrhea, bad breath, sugar cravings, food allergies or sensitivities, moodiness, anxiety, depression, skin issues (such as eczema), or the inability to lose weight.

Now that we have addressed overall gut health, I want to dive deeper into how an overgrowth of bad bacteria in the gut can be related to depression, anxiety and so many more mental health issues.

*Studies show that the brain is connected to the gut not just by physical symptoms, but also emotional. It is very common that bad gut bacteria lead to depressive like behaviors as well as anxiety.*

Researchers from University of Virginia released a study Spring of 2017 that addresses gut bacteria in mice and how it correlates to their behavior. In short, their findings proved that getting the right bacteria in the gut changed the behavior of the mice. They showed that the mice with better gut health (aka the right probiotics) were more active, did not appear "depressed," and would swim longer before giving up when submerged in water.

Studies show that the brain is connected to the gut not just by physical symptoms, but also emotional. It is very common that bad gut bacteria lead to depressive like behaviors as well as anxiety. So, obviously, with Think Fit Method, we are working hard to address mental barriers to health and wellness and that is why gut health is so important.

Chief Nutritionist, Charity Lighten, from Silver Fern Brand states:
"Healthy bacteria help create vitamins for the body, strengthen the immune system, kill pathogens and keep our gut lining strong. They also play a huge role in brain health. The "gut-brain" connection refers to the constant communication that is going

on between your gut and your brain. We now know that the gut is filled with neurons that are designed to send messages to the brain (and vice versa).

This means that our brain health is also heavily linked to what's going on in the gut. And not just physical aspect, emotional issues can also affect both our gut AND our brain."

## SO THEN HOW DO WE GET THIS BAD BACTERIA OUT AND THE HEALTHY BACTERIA IN?

First, like I stated above, PROBIOTICS! The right probiotic is key. One that will sustain all the way down to the large and small intestines. The good bacteria will feed off of the prebiotic fibers in probiotics, as well as when you eat a diet high in fiber from healthy foods.

Next, it is imperative to avoid simple sugars which feeds the bad bacteria.

And lastly, you need to de-stress. Having high cortisol levels in the body can feed into that bad bacteria in your gut making for so many more issues. So take a minute, recognize your stress levels and then set aside some time to de-stress. Your gut will thank you! Now see page 93 to complete worksheet 5:2.

Resources

Body Weight Misperception in Adolescence and Incident Obesity in Young Adulthood - Angelina R. Sutin, Antonio Terracciano, 2015. (2018). Retrieved from http://journals.sagepub.com/doi/abs/10.1177/0956797614566319

UVA Reverses Depression Symptoms in Mice Using Probiotics. (2018). Retrieved from https://news.virginia.edu/content/uva-reverses-depression-symptoms-mice-using-probiotics

Krishnan, K. (2017). Silver Fern™ Brand | Gut Health, Probiotics, Prebiotics, and More. [online] SilverFernBrand.com. Available at: https://www.silverfernbrand.com/

UVA Today. (2018). UVA Reverses Depression Symptoms in Mice Using Probiotics. [online] Available at: https://news.virginia.edu/content/uva-reverses-depression-symptoms-mice-using-probiotics

Lighten, C. (2017). Silver Fern™ Brand | Gut Health, Probiotics, Prebiotics, and More. [online] SilverFernBrand.com. Available at: https://www.silverfernbrand.com/

# Overcoming Negative Self Talk

## Observe your thoughts and write them down.

Spend 5 minutes monitoring your thoughts about yourself. What do you think of yourself? It is extremely important to be aware of what negative thoughts are going through your brain. Write them down.

## Write down your triggers.

Spend 5 more minutes thinking about what triggers lead you to think these negative things. Write them down. Understanding and bringing into awareness the things that trigger you is very important in changing your thought behavior.

## Close your eyes and choose your mantra for the day.

Say this OUT LOUD to yourself repeatedly throughout the day. Some examples are: "You're beautiful," "You can do this," "You will succeed today," "I am happy today," "I am beautiful the way I am." As you go about your day, have this on repeat both silently in your head and out loud so your ears hear it.

## Make it a game.

Instead of telling yourself "I will never lose this weight," tell yourself "I can lose this weight, just watch." Challenge yourself in this game and prove yourself wrong while stopping the black and white thinking. Stop using the words "never" or "always." Prove yourself wrong. Write it down:

## Turn the negative into a positive & make a gratitude list.

Make a list of 10 things you are grateful for and keep it with you all the time. A great place to put this is in your purse or stuck to your computer where you work all day. Every time a negative thought comes into your mind about yourself, take out the paper and speak OUT LOUD the things you are grateful for and what you are celebrating. Write these 10 things down here:

1.

2.

3.

4.

5.

6.

7.

8.

9.

10.

Positive circle.

It is said that we are the average of the 5 people we spend the most time with. So write down the most positive thinkers in your life. Make these your people.

As you can see, retraining that negative self talk really starts with identifying the problem and then retraining yourself to speak positive things. By speaking out loud, your ears are hearing this and you will begin to retrain your brain to think those things instead of negative things.

THINK FIT METHOD *tip*

A negative mindset and negative self talk is detrimental in your weight loss journey and can set you back. So take some time today to start creating a new habit and creating new neuro-pathways of thinking. This takes time and requires work, but I can promise you in the end, it will be worth the journey.

# Foods to Consume

## WHAT FOODS DID GOD INTEND US TO CONSUME?

*"Then God said, "Behold, I have given you every plant yielding seed that is on the surface of all the earth, and every tree which has fruit yielding seed; it shall be food for you." Genesis 1:29 NASB*

Rewrite the verse above:

Re-read the verse out loud. Meditate on this verse. What does it mean to you?

Let me tell you what it means to me. When God created man, along with the heavens and the earth, He also created food. Plants, fruits, and animals for man to consume. He did not create the modified food that we now have today. So when you are thinking about sugar, ask yourself, did God intend for me to consume this?

How do you feel your sugar intake is on a scale from 1-10?

How can you limit/eliminate these high sugar foods/ drinks you consume? What are some common things you eat that are high in sugar?

How would you rate your overall gut health on a scale from 1-10?

Do you struggle with any of these common signs of poor gut health:

Digestive issues such as constipation, bloating, gas or diarrhea, bad breath, sugar cravings, food allergies or sensitivities, moodiness, anxiety, depression, skin issues (such as eczema), or the inability to lose weight

What are some foods you consume that could be feeding the bad bacteria in your gut?

What foods are you going to start eliminating this week?

# Weekly Reflection

What were the biggest revelations and lessons learned this week?

What are you grateful for this past week?

List three positives of the week when it comes to your nutrition and exercise journey:

1.

2.

3.

List three things you would like to improve on next week. What concrete actions can you take to work towards these?

1.

2.

3.

How did you stop negative self talk this week?

How can you apply this verse moving forward on this journey?

What changes did you make to promote a healthy gut this week? List as many as applicable:

# WEEK FIVE DEVOTIONS

Luke 10:27

[27] He answered, "'Love the Lord
your God with all your heart and
with all your soul and with all
your strength and with all your
mind'[a]; and, 'Love your neighbor
as yourself.

*W*e all have two Pandora stations in our heads...one is KLOVE and the other is known as KSCREW radio. When we enter into negative self-talk we are tearing ourselves down and it usually is associated to self-worth and our mindset. Earlier we looked at our self-worth and mindset, so for this lesson we will focus on how to tune into KLOVE radio more frequently. Some of these versus we have looked at earlier, however they are so important to help us move past this bondage of negative thought patterns!

Friends, if you recall **Luke 10:27** we are to love our neighbors as ourselves. I am not sure about you, but I've heard a message for many years to put others first, to walk humbly, to serve others before myself. This message somehow, I think has been interpreted differently than the intention. The human side of us does put ego in the way; however when we feel rooted and spiritually connected to God who is leading us and are led and infused with His Holy Spirit (**Acts 1:8**) we are confident in His love and His provisions. With the Holy Spirit in us, how can we not love ourselves? When we love ourselves, we can treat our neighbors with love and compassion, truly wanting them to go first, to have the best and to serve them because it helps them, not because we feel compelled to follow a rule! The fruit of the Spirit will be shining through us and we will be free of the burden of our negative self-talk! Christ wants us to be free and serve others out of love. Friends, continue to seek and build your spiritual connection to God and the fruits and KLOVE radio will continue to expand not only in our actions but in our minds!!

**Read Galatians 5** - This chapter is filled with wisdom! Expressing our faith in love means loving who we are – made in God's image (remember, God isn't made in our image, but rather we are made to reflect Him!). **Utilize your journal,** jotting down thoughts you have around these perspectives.

**Pray and meditate** on how you exhibit the fruit of the Spirit. Do a gut check, listing the fruit (love, joy, peace, patience, kindness, goodness, faithfulness, gentleness and self-control) and jot down how and when you last experienced these. See any trends or themes? Make notes...

Now look at the five people you listed who support you– how do they show themselves and others the fruit of the Spirit? **Write** a prayer in your journal asking God to continue to infuse His Spirit in you and to keep your mind open to opportunities to share those fruits with yourself and others!

**Read Psalms 139:5-12.** When we do enter into negative self-talk sometimes we need a reminder that God is with us – no matter where we go!!

How does knowing God is with you always, even in the darkness, provide you assurance?

Reflect on other times you have been in the heat of negativity and found God's hand guiding you. Take a moment to jot down what resonates with you in your **journal.**

Notice over the following days when you find yourself tuning into KSCREW radio – what is happening? What are you doing? How or what are you feeling when you start this station up and spiral into negativity? Look at your food log – are there certain foods, activities or yes, even

*Digging Deeper*

*Take a piece of paper, decorating it however you want – stickers, drawings, markers, colored pencils...whatever you find appealing. Write Psalms 118:24 on this piece of paper and hang it somewhere (your bathroom mirror is a good place) so you can reaffirm that this truly is a day the Lord has made and you can rejoice knowing you are His! Starting your day with a positive mindset does wonders for which station we will tune into!*

friends that trigger this? Once you are aware, then you can start to face these thoughts, activities and even friends with confidence and the power of the Holy Spirit! **Utilize your journal** to make note of any awareness you have!

*Journal it!*

_____

_____

_____

_____

If you are in need of a workout plan or nutrition guidance, please jump in to my next virtual bootcamp at jennymire.com or take advantage of the full Think Fit Method portal at thinkfitmethod.com

# MONDAY - TRACK YOUR WORKOUT

Exercise: _____

*Rate how you feel*

| Before Workout: | 1 | 2 | 3 | 4 | 5 | 6 | 7 | 8 | 9 | 10 |
|---|---|---|---|---|---|---|---|---|---|---|
| During Workout: | 1 | 2 | 3 | 4 | 5 | 6 | 7 | 8 | 9 | 10 |
| After Workout: | 1 | 2 | 3 | 4 | 5 | 6 | 7 | 8 | 9 | 10 |

Total exercise time: _____  Approximate Calories Burned: _____

Water Goal (oz): _____  Water Consumed (oz): _____

*Today My Win Was:* _____
*Tomorrow I Will:* _____

# TUESDAY - TRACK YOUR WORKOUT

Exercise: _____

*Rate how you feel*

| Before Workout: | 1 | 2 | 3 | 4 | 5 | 6 | 7 | 8 | 9 | 10 |
|---|---|---|---|---|---|---|---|---|---|---|
| During Workout: | 1 | 2 | 3 | 4 | 5 | 6 | 7 | 8 | 9 | 10 |
| After Workout: | 1 | 2 | 3 | 4 | 5 | 6 | 7 | 8 | 9 | 10 |

Total exercise time: _____  Approximate Calories Burned: _____

Water Goal (oz): _____  Water Consumed (oz): _____

*Today My Win Was:* _____
*Tomorrow I Will:* _____

# WEDNESDAY - TRACK YOUR WORKOUT

Exercise: _____

## Rate how you feel

| Before Workout: | 1 | 2 | 3 | 4 | 5 | 6 | 7 | 8 | 9 | 10 |
|---|---|---|---|---|---|---|---|---|---|---|

| During Workout: | 1 | 2 | 3 | 4 | 5 | 6 | 7 | 8 | 9 | 10 |
|---|---|---|---|---|---|---|---|---|---|---|

| After Workout: | 1 | 2 | 3 | 4 | 5 | 6 | 7 | 8 | 9 | 10 |
|---|---|---|---|---|---|---|---|---|---|---|

Total exercise time: _____    Approximate Calories Burned: _____

Water Goal (oz): _____    Water Consumed (oz): _____

Today My Win Was: _____

Tomorrow I Will: _____

# THURSDAY - TRACK YOUR WORKOUT

Exercise: _____

## Rate how you feel

| Before Workout: | 1 | 2 | 3 | 4 | 5 | 6 | 7 | 8 | 9 | 10 |
|---|---|---|---|---|---|---|---|---|---|---|

| During Workout: | 1 | 2 | 3 | 4 | 5 | 6 | 7 | 8 | 9 | 10 |
|---|---|---|---|---|---|---|---|---|---|---|

| After Workout: | 1 | 2 | 3 | 4 | 5 | 6 | 7 | 8 | 9 | 10 |
|---|---|---|---|---|---|---|---|---|---|---|

Total exercise time: _____    Approximate Calories Burned: _____

Water Goal (oz): _____    Water Consumed (oz): _____

Today My Win Was: _____

Tomorrow I Will: _____

# **FRIDAY** - TRACK YOUR WORKOUT

Exercise: _____

## Rate how you feel

| Before Workout: | 1 | 2 | 3 | 4 | 5 | 6 | 7 | 8 | 9 | 10 |
|---|---|---|---|---|---|---|---|---|---|---|

| During Workout: | 1 | 2 | 3 | 4 | 5 | 6 | 7 | 8 | 9 | 10 |
|---|---|---|---|---|---|---|---|---|---|---|

| After Workout: | 1 | 2 | 3 | 4 | 5 | 6 | 7 | 8 | 9 | 10 |
|---|---|---|---|---|---|---|---|---|---|---|

Total exercise time: _____    Approximate Calories Burned: _____

Water Goal (oz): _____    Water Consumed (oz): _____

Today My Win Was: _____

Tomorrow I Will: _____

# **WEEKEND** - TRACK YOUR WORKOUT

Exercise: _____

## Rate how you feel

| Before Workout: | 1 | 2 | 3 | 4 | 5 | 6 | 7 | 8 | 9 | 10 |
|---|---|---|---|---|---|---|---|---|---|---|

| During Workout: | 1 | 2 | 3 | 4 | 5 | 6 | 7 | 8 | 9 | 10 |
|---|---|---|---|---|---|---|---|---|---|---|

| After Workout: | 1 | 2 | 3 | 4 | 5 | 6 | 7 | 8 | 9 | 10 |
|---|---|---|---|---|---|---|---|---|---|---|

Total exercise time: _____    Approximate Calories Burned: _____

Water Goal (oz): _____    Water Consumed (oz): _____

Today My Win Was: _____

Tomorrow I Will: _____

COMPARISON &
STRATEGIC EXERCISE

6

# WEEK
# SIX

# COMPARISON + STRATEGIC EXERCISE

*"For am I now seeking the favor of men, or of God? Or am I striving to please men? If I were still trying to please men, I would not be a bondservant of Christ."*
*Galatians 1:10*

The comparison game is a strong one. And we, as women, often find ourselves struggling with this each and every day. With how prevalent social media is in this day and age, we see the "ideal" body everywhere, right? It is thrown in our faces and what scares me the most is that our daughters and sons will have it a thousand times worse than we do. So we must acknowledge this issue of the heart and mind in ourselves so that we can, in turn, help our children.

When you start to compare yourself with others, your insecurities will come on full force. But God didn't intend for that. He tells us to only seek approval from Him, not to seek approval from men.

2 Corinthians 10:12 (ESV) tells us, "Not that we dare to classify or compare ourselves with some of those who are commending themselves. But when they measure themselves by one another and compare themselves with one another, they are without understanding."

Here are some of the top ways I see women comparing themselves to other women:

**The way their body looks.** This happens to the best of us - looking at another woman and wishing you looked like that. Maybe she is naturally thinner than you are. Maybe she has the muscle definition you wish you had. Maybe you want her curves. Whatever it is, we have all been there.

**How "put together" they are.** You see a woman who appears to have it all together... the perfect husband, the perfect house, the most well behaved kids, the perfect career and the grass looks greener on the other side, right? Wrong. No matter how put together you think another woman is, I promise you she has her own chaos in her life as well.

**Their social media page.** So you see a photo of an "instagram worthy" home or a photo with the perfect lighting to show off their obliques. You wish you had their skills for social media right? Their ability to get 200k followers. And it eats at you... how come they can do it and I can't? We begin to question ourselves and our "worthiness."

**How exciting or adventurous their life looks.** Maybe you see it on social media or maybe you see it in your friends' lives, but you wish you could have just a little of the excitement they have. You compare your "boring" life with theirs and think it's just not fair.

We can so easily fall into the trap of comparing our lives to others that we begin to only live for a social media post and how it is represented on social media rather than simply enjoying the moment.

Theodore Roosevelt simply stated that "comparison is the thief of joy" and this couldn't be closer to the truth. When we constantly compare ourselves with those people who we THINK to be better than we are, we are robbing ourselves of truly living in the joy of our lives that God intended. But not only does comparison steal joy, it can destroy confidence, self worth, and ruin relationships.

> *Comparison steals our energy and time. This is time and energy you could be putting in to living YOUR best life.*

**Some way that comparison can destroy are:**
1. Comparison steals our energy and time. This is time and energy you could be putting in to living YOUR best life.
2. Comparison does not lead to happiness. Nothing about comparing your life or your body to someone else will lead to you being happy. It is a losing game. Trust that God has you where He wants you and strive to please HIM, and Him alone.
3. Comparison is based on what you perceive and FEEL, and not the truth. You do not know what is really happening in someone else's life or heart. Social media does NOT always tell the truth my friends. The grass is NOT always greener on the other side - the grass is GREENER where you water it. So focus on YOU.
4. Comparison discredits our own achievements. The more you compare, the more you think you are not enough. And this couldn't be further from the truth. Remember back to week 1 when we talked about your worth? YOU ARE WORTH IT and YOU ARE ENOUGH.
5. Comparison ruins relationships. When you look at someone else and think they have it all, you taint your relationship with them. Jealousy comes in and is an ugly thing.

*"Do nothing from selfishness or empty conceit, but with humility of mind regard one another as more important than yourselves; do not merely look out for your own personal interests, but also for the interests of others." Philippians 2:3-4*

Remember, God did not call us to compare ourselves with others but rather focus on Him and loving others. He sums it up pretty well in one of the ten commandments.

*"You shall not covet your neighbor's house; you shall not covet your neighbor's wife or his male servant or his female servant or his ox or his donkey or anything that belongs to your neighbor." Exodus 20:17*

Let's now address how we work on stopping the comparison game. Head over to worksheet 6:1 and complete.

## STRATEGIC EXERCISE

Comparison is huge in the fitness world and I see this all too often. But comparison is only one of the lies the fitness industry tells. Another lie the fitness industry tells us is that in order to lose weight, we have to do massive amounts of cardio. We need to spend hours a week on the treadmill running endless miles to get the body composition that we're craving. But hours on end doing cardio isn't going to get you where you want to be, not effectively, and not on its own.

*Ladies, let me tell you, in order to get the results you want, you must lift weights.*

Gone are the days of long drawn out cardio. And thank goodness for that. Over the past decade, more and more research shows that strength training can be beneficial for not only gaining muscle tone, but losing fat as well. That is what I base all of my programing around.

Why are you scared to lift? In general, women tend to be scared of lifting weights. I hear it all the time with clients. And being the owner of a gym, I constantly sit and watch the majority of women spend hours on the elliptical or treadmill with little to no change after months and months of cardio.

**The top three things I hear from women about why they don't want to lift weights are:**

"I don't want to get bulky and look like a man"

"I don't know what I'm doing and the men in there intimidate me"

"Lifting weights won't help me lose weight"

## LET'S NOW ADDRESS THESE THINGS.

1. "I don't want to get bulky and look like a man." There truly is only one way to get "bulky" and "look like a man" and that is to take steroids or testosterone supplementation. Women do not produce the same level of testosterone as men do in order to truly bulk up. Lifting heavy weights will tone and increase strength in women, not increase size. So don't stress about looking like a man! It won't happen.

2. "I don't know what I'm doing and the men intimidate me." I get this. I understand this feeling of walking into a gym and not knowing what to do. If you feel like this, have someone teach you what to do in a weight room. The best thing a woman can do for herself at the gym is to have a basic knowledge of how to function in a weight room and how to lift properly. Don't let this be your excuse to not lift weights. Hire a trainer for a few sessions to teach you what to do. Nothing is better than walking into a new gym (on vacation or wherever) and knowing what you are doing. Don't be intimidated by those men in there – just walk in there with confidence and DO YOUR THING ladies!

3. "Lifting weights won't help me lose weight." This couldn't be further from the truth! Muscle is imperative to help you lose weight and keep the weight off. Muscles increase and ramp up your metabolism. One pound of muscle can burn up to 20 calories per day whereas one pound of fat only burns 5 calories per day. When you add weight training into your workout, you continue to burn calories long after your workout is over. So over time, you will lose weight! But always remember... you cannot out exercise a bad diet. So keep that nutrition in check!

Strength training is critical to building muscle, while isometric training is critical to shaping muscles to give them a longer, leaner look. Strength training alone tends to build the larger muscle groups in your body. Doing other types of exercise like Pilates and Barre, utilizes isometric movements that shape different muscles in your body. While strength training alone will help you speed up your metabolism and shed unwanted body fat, adding in isometric movement on a regular basis will help you to more holistically shape your body. So I recommend throwing in a little Barre, Pilates or Yoga when you can.

Now let's dig a little bit into the most effective exercise strategies. HIIT (High Intensity Interval Training) is a workout focused on intensity training with alternating intervals of all-out-high-intensity-work and low intensity rest periods. HIIT workouts can be done in all kinds of formats: with equipment or without, in the gym or at home, body weight or weights, machines or pavement. The main point of HIIT training is to train in intervals of different speeds (allowing for your heart rate to vary) and never allowing your body to adjust to that speed.

Working out obviously burns calories, however, HIIT burns calories long after your workout is done. This occurs because of the way your body utilizes oxygen during your high intensity work periods. Simply put, this is called excess post-exercise oxygen consumption, or EPOC. EPOC is the amount of oxygen required to restore your body to its normal, resting level of metabolic function (called homeostasis). This is how your body continues to burn calories for hours (or even days) after you have finished your HIIT workout.

## HOW IS EPOC CREATED?

We are using energy all the time to keep our bodies going. When we exercise, we use more energy, and we create a need for more energy. We need to repair our muscles, we need to remove lactic acid from those muscles, we need to replace the energy we lost during our workout, and all of these things take Oxygen. The more we need our bodies to work after a workout to get back into a natural state, the bigger the EPOC effect is.

Cardio alone does not create much EPOC. By the time you've grabbed your bag and walked out to your car, you're done burning excess calories. This doesn't mean that cardio is a waste of time, it does however mean that you're not going to get the most out of your time at the gym if all you're doing is cardio. Cardio is not working large muscle groups to their maximum, and it doesn't create the need to majorly 'repair' afterwards. This is the main reason why cardio is not going to help you shed the extra weight as fast and the main reason I have my clients focus on HIIT workouts and cardio.

*Studies have shown that doing just a few sprints 3 times per week burns more fat after 6 weeks than doing 60 minutes of steady state-cardio (walking on an inclined treadmill) 3 times per week.*

Research has also shown that HIIT workouts increase your body's resting metabolic rate for up to 24 hours after your workout is complete. This means that your metabolism speeds up for 24 hours after your HIIT workout. That sounds pretty great, doesn't it?

HIIT also helps you lose belly fat (you know, that stubborn fat around your midsection that you just can't seem to get rid of). The most common HIIT exercise I have my clients do is sprinting. We focus on an all out sprint (or max effort) for about 20 seconds, and then recover for nearly 40 seconds by jogging or just resting in general.

Studies have shown that doing just a few sprints 3 times per week burns more fat after 6 weeks than doing 60 minutes of steady state-cardio (walking on an inclined treadmill) 3 times per week. In addition, 20 minutes of HIIT, 3 times a week, was shown to significantly lower a participant's belly fat.

But not only does it help with metabolism and fat burn, HIIT requires your heart muscle to work under high demands. This strengthens the heart, lowers blood pressure and improves aerobic performance overall.

I am often asked by clients how long it takes to start seeing results. This often comes from people who are expecting fat to melt off quickly once they start making changes. Unfortunately, there is no quick fix. Real change takes time and lots of work...but is totally worth it!

## RESULTS ARE DIFFERENT FOR EVERYONE.

Depending on your starting point, you may begin seeing some immediate changes. If you have a lot of weight to lose, you typically see change happen quickly once you begin to dial in your nutrition and exercise. However, there is no real set time period for seeing results when you are talking about physical results. Some people see small changes in as little as 1 week, while it takes others 3-4 weeks to see any real changes. However, you should notice some non-scale victories within a couple of weeks of cleaning up your diet and working out.

## IT TOOK TIME TO PUT WEIGHT ON, IT WILL TAKE TIME TO TAKE IT OFF.

You didn't gain that extra 20 pounds overnight...so you won't take it off overnight. In order to lose one pound of weight, you need to cut 3500 calories. If you want to sustain your weight loss over time, then simply restricting your calories is NOT an effective strategy. Instead, you need to cycle your calories and macronutrients so that

*If you want to sustain your weight loss over time, then simply restricting your calories is NOT an effective strategy. Instead, you need to cycle your calories and macronutrients so that you don't create a lower set point for your metabolism.*

you don't create a lower set point for your metabolism. That takes a bit more time and intentionality, but will truly pay off in the long run. Taking your time with your weight loss ensures you won't yo-yo back after a crash diet messes with your metabolic rate! If you want to see real results that last, you are going to have to make changes to how you live and build consistency with those new habits. That won't happen in a week, but can happen as early as 3-4 weeks into the program. However, the real change may not happen until a couple of months into your health and fitness journey, once you've created ingrained habits that allow your body to function optimally.

Results can happen shortly after starting a new health and fitness regimen, no doubt, but real results that last and can be sustained over time will take longer. Those kinds of results will require hard work, accountability, encouragement and intentionality. While the progress toward those goals may seem slower, it will actually get you to your goal more effectively. And that is what we are doing in Think Fit Method™.

Nutrition and intentional exercise go hand in hand in order to get results. Let's briefly dive in to the why and how - there will be more on this in the next section.

When you strength train, your body needs carbohydrates to fuel your muscles; but on the other hand, it is known that some carbs spike insulin levels, which essentially feeds our body fat. So with cycling our carbohydrate intake, we are eliminating that fat storing process. We do this by strength training on certain days where we have more complex carbs. When we do that, we are replenishing glycogen stores and preserving/building our muscles at the same time! In short, the higher/regular complex carbs on training days go right to our muscles instead of being converted to fat stores.

Lower carb days are designed for a full depletion of carbohydrates in our bodies. Workouts are geared towards burst training, thus utilizing all the glycogen stores in our bodies. During these workouts, we begin to use more fat as fuel opposed to carbs. On lower carb days, the primary focus is fat BURN, not muscle growth. You are utilizing all the built up carbs/calories from higher carb day and essentially are in fat burning mode 24/7.

This pattern tricks your metabolism into burning fat all the time. It is a proven process and shows some amazing results. In order to lose weight, our bodies need the right combo of carbs, healthy fats and proteins, and on my carb cycling plan you learn that perfect combination to make you a fat burning furnace!

Now that we talked about strategic exercise, I want to remind you that everyone starts somewhere. Every person is at different levels with their exercise. So please don't compare yourself to the other girl at the gym that is lifting heavier than you or running faster than you. Focus on YOU and give it 100% and the results will come.

Resources
McCall, P. (2018). 7 Things to Know About Excess Post-exercise Oxygen Consumption (EPOC). [online] Acefitness.org. Available at: https://www.acefitness.org/education-and-resources/professional/expert-articles/5008/7-things-to-know-about-excess-post-exercise-oxygen-consumption-epoc [Accessed 6 Aug. 2018].

# Stop the Comparison Game

What things do you find yourself comparing to others about? List them here.

What do you want YOUR life to look like?

Can you change your life to ultimately get to where you want to be? If so, what can you change?

What is your attitude towards others whom you perceive to have what you want?

How can you change that attitude to focus on you?

THINK FIT METHOD *tip*

It's time to start focusing on what you DO have instead of what you DON'T have. You are here, in Think Fit MethodTM, because you are wanting to change your life. Remember, it starts with YOU. It starts in your heart and in your mind. Be proud of where you have come the past few weeks and stop looking at others and comparing your journey to their journeys. Everyone is different. Focus on YOU and the reward will be there.

# *Weekly Reflection*

What were the biggest revelations and lessons learned this week?

What are you grateful for this past week?

List three positives of the week when it comes to your nutrition and exercise journey:

1.

2.

3.

List three things you would like to improve on next week.
What concrete actions can you take to work towards these?

1.

2.

3.

When did you catch yourself in the comparison game this week? And how did you overcome it?

From 1-10, how do you feel you did this week?

What does Galatians 1:10 mean to you this week?

*"For am I now seeking the favor of men, or of God? Or am I striving to please men? If I were still trying to please men, I would not be a bondservant of Christ." Galatians 1:10*

How can you apply this verse moving forward on this journey?

# WEEK SIX DEVOTIONS

Romans 15:1-2, 7

[1] We who are strong ought to bear with the failings of the weak and not to please ourselves. [2] Each of us should please our neighbors for their good, to build them up.

[7] Accept one another, then, just as Christ accepted you, in order to bring praise to God.

*F*riends, as we look at comparison it is important you know my heart. I do have a belief that breaks down pretty simply that most, if not all, our actions come from a place of fear or a place of love. You can almost do the why exercise with any behavior to get to the intention of that action occurring because you feared something or because you were acting in love. This is a daily struggle for me to ensure I'm praying AND listening to God, so I can bear the fruit of the Spirit to myself and those around me. Why do I need to explain this? Comparison of ourselves, really when we break it down – well, doesn't it come from a place of fear? I'm not using comparison to say I'm comparing some numbers for my business or flooring to go in my house. Please understand, comparing ourselves, bodies, minds, spirits, and hearts really is judgement. It may be judgment of others or of ourselves, but either way typically manifests itself in such ways as jealousy, resentfulness, coveting, envy or even boastfulness. This creates that KSCREW radio we discussed in the last section which then binds us in chains.

**Read Romans 15:1-2 and 7.** As we learn to take care of our bodies with healthy eating and exercise why wouldn't we want to share with others?

Take a few moments and think of a time when you were struggling, and others had the miracle answer to what you needed to do. What was the impact on you? Sometimes it leads us in the right direction and other times it doesn't. What's the difference or is there?

How can I support others who have had success while I am starting or continuing my health journey? How do I keep in mind what others might need versus my need to share because of my excitement?

How can I glorify God when I share my journey? How can I be aware of where I'm at in my journey? How can I be aware of where others are at in their journey and offer the type of encouragement they need?

How can we accept ourselves right where we are at knowing that God loves us and because He abides in us we have this divine love for ourselves? (Remember Luke 10:27? Now **Read I Corinthians 3: 16**)

Each of us were made very differently. Our look, skin tone, shape, size and how we carry ourselves. Why would we think then that we should look like someone else?

Earlier in the journal you listed out those items you loved about yourself. Go back to that and now add 5 more items. Is it your heart for Jesus? Is it your skin has cleared up as you have started drinking more water? They do not need to be mountain moving items...each area that we start to love ourselves with God's love, leads us to STOP comparing ourselves to others.

## Digging Deep

*Take some time to pray and meditate asking God to show you where you might be comparing yourself to others, not feeling worthy of the goal set before you on your health journey. After completing this, go deeper on the question that is asked in worksheet 6:1 on page 113. What do you want your life to look like?*

*Let's break it down a bit by looking at our mental, physical, spiritual, and emotional health. Take the time to really write it out and describe it...feel it. Use your senses to get started by answering the following questions for each.*

*What does being mentally healthy look like for me? What does it feel like? How does it impact my relationship with God and my relationship with others? What does it smell like? (yes, stretch yourself a bit here please) What does it taste like? I know this sounds wonky and to give you an example the first time I did this I struggled...when I prayed and asked God these questions the idea of coaching others to find their greatest calling tasted like mint! Refreshing and invigorating!*

*After answering the questions, take some time to reread what you wrote and notice any areas that might be emerging for you, noting these in your journal. Remember, defining what we want is important because we focus on what we define. If we only define what we don't want, guess what happens?*

Journal it!

If you are in need of a workout plan or nutrition guidance, please jump in to my next virtual bootcamp at jennymire.com or take advantage of the full Think Fit Method portal at thinkfitmethod.com

# **MONDAY** - TRACK YOUR WORKOUT

Exercise: _____

*Rate how you feel*

| Before Workout: | 1 | 2 | 3 | 4 | 5 | 6 | 7 | 8 | 9 | 10 |
|---|---|---|---|---|---|---|---|---|---|---|

| During Workout: | 1 | 2 | 3 | 4 | 5 | 6 | 7 | 8 | 9 | 10 |
|---|---|---|---|---|---|---|---|---|---|---|

| After Workout: | 1 | 2 | 3 | 4 | 5 | 6 | 7 | 8 | 9 | 10 |
|---|---|---|---|---|---|---|---|---|---|---|

Total exercise time: _____   Approximate Calories Burned: _____

Water Goal (oz): _____   Water Consumed (oz): _____

*Today My Win Was:* _____

*Tomorrow I Will:* _____

# **TUESDAY** - TRACK YOUR WORKOUT

Exercise: _____

*Rate how you feel*

| Before Workout: | 1 | 2 | 3 | 4 | 5 | 6 | 7 | 8 | 9 | 10 |
|---|---|---|---|---|---|---|---|---|---|---|

| During Workout: | 1 | 2 | 3 | 4 | 5 | 6 | 7 | 8 | 9 | 10 |
|---|---|---|---|---|---|---|---|---|---|---|

| After Workout: | 1 | 2 | 3 | 4 | 5 | 6 | 7 | 8 | 9 | 10 |
|---|---|---|---|---|---|---|---|---|---|---|

Total exercise time: _____   Approximate Calories Burned: _____

Water Goal (oz): _____   Water Consumed (oz): _____

*Today My Win Was:* _____

*Tomorrow I Will:* _____

# **WEDNESDAY** - TRACK YOUR WORKOUT

Exercise: _____

## *Rate how you feel*

| Before Workout: | 1 | 2 | 3 | 4 | 5 | 6 | 7 | 8 | 9 | 10 |
|---|---|---|---|---|---|---|---|---|---|---|

| During Workout: | 1 | 2 | 3 | 4 | 5 | 6 | 7 | 8 | 9 | 10 |
|---|---|---|---|---|---|---|---|---|---|---|

| After Workout: | 1 | 2 | 3 | 4 | 5 | 6 | 7 | 8 | 9 | 10 |
|---|---|---|---|---|---|---|---|---|---|---|

Total exercise time: _____     Approximate Calories Burned: _____

Water Goal (oz): _____     Water Consumed (oz): _____

*Today My Win Was:* _____

*Tomorrow I Will:* _____

# **THURSDAY** - TRACK YOUR WORKOUT

Exercise: _____

## *Rate how you feel*

| Before Workout: | 1 | 2 | 3 | 4 | 5 | 6 | 7 | 8 | 9 | 10 |
|---|---|---|---|---|---|---|---|---|---|---|

| During Workout: | 1 | 2 | 3 | 4 | 5 | 6 | 7 | 8 | 9 | 10 |
|---|---|---|---|---|---|---|---|---|---|---|

| After Workout: | 1 | 2 | 3 | 4 | 5 | 6 | 7 | 8 | 9 | 10 |
|---|---|---|---|---|---|---|---|---|---|---|

Total exercise time: _____     Approximate Calories Burned: _____

Water Goal (oz): _____     Water Consumed (oz): _____

*Today My Win Was:* _____

*Tomorrow I Will:* _____

# **FRIDAY** - TRACK YOUR WORKOUT

Exercise: _____

*Rate how you feel*

| Before Workout: | 1 | 2 | 3 | 4 | 5 | 6 | 7 | 8 | 9 | 10 |
|---|---|---|---|---|---|---|---|---|---|---|

| During Workout: | 1 | 2 | 3 | 4 | 5 | 6 | 7 | 8 | 9 | 10 |
|---|---|---|---|---|---|---|---|---|---|---|

| After Workout: | 1 | 2 | 3 | 4 | 5 | 6 | 7 | 8 | 9 | 10 |
|---|---|---|---|---|---|---|---|---|---|---|

Total exercise time: _____    Approximate Calories Burned: _____

Water Goal (oz): _____    Water Consumed (oz): _____

*Today My Win Was:* _____

*Tomorrow I Will:* _____

# **WEEKEND** - TRACK YOUR WORKOUT

Exercise: _____

*Rate how you feel*

| Before Workout: | 1 | 2 | 3 | 4 | 5 | 6 | 7 | 8 | 9 | 10 |
|---|---|---|---|---|---|---|---|---|---|---|

| During Workout: | 1 | 2 | 3 | 4 | 5 | 6 | 7 | 8 | 9 | 10 |
|---|---|---|---|---|---|---|---|---|---|---|

| After Workout: | 1 | 2 | 3 | 4 | 5 | 6 | 7 | 8 | 9 | 10 |
|---|---|---|---|---|---|---|---|---|---|---|

Total exercise time: _____    Approximate Calories Burned: _____

Water Goal (oz): _____    Water Consumed (oz): _____

*Today My Win Was:* _____

*Tomorrow I Will:* _____

GAINING PEACE &
INTENTIONAL NUTRITION

7

# WEEK
# SEVEN

*"Be anxious for nothing, but in everything by prayer and supplication with thanksgiving let your requests be made known to God. And the peace of God which surpasses all comprehension, will guard your hearts and your minds in Christ Jesus." Philippians 4:6-7*

*G*aining peace in a world full of chaos can be hard to say the least. And gaining peace in terms of your health and wellness journey is even harder. Often times we find ourselves fretting over the small things and our anxiety takes over. But God calls us to let go of the anxiety. Easier said than done, right?

*"Therefore humble yourselves under the mighty hand of God, that He may exalt you at the proper time, casting all your anxiety on Him, because He cares for you." 1 Peter 5:6-7*

God calls us to trust Him. He wants us to have peace in our hearts. So I challenge you today to pray a prayer of peace. Pray that He gives you peace with whatever you are going through in life. When you gain that peace, you will be able to really address this health journey you so long for.

Many people (much more than you may realize) struggle with anxiety to some degree or another, especially when it comes to weight loss. Not knowing exactly what to do. Being overwhelmed by all the information out there. Stressing about everything they eat. The struggle is real. And the struggle is hard.

Webster's dictionary definition of anxiety is:
*"apprehensive uneasiness or nervousness usually over an impending or anticipated ill";*
        or
*"an abnormal and overwhelming sense of apprehension and fear often marked by physical signs (such as tension, sweating, and increased pulse rate), by doubt concerning the reality and nature of the threat, and by self-doubt about one's capacity to cope with it."*

This week I want to equip you with tools that will help you plan for the outer work you are doing which will in turn support the inner work of peace. Finding peace with yourself is one of the first steps, as we addressed earlier in this journal, so now it is time to address the plan that will help lessen the anxiety.

Head over to worksheet 7:1 on page 131.

## INTENTIONAL NUTRITION

Eating intentionally can play such a huge role in your overall health and wellness. I want to discuss the main points for you to focus on when it comes to nutrition. So let's dive in to what macronutrients are and why you need them.

I'm sure you've heard the term "macros" a lot in today's world and a lot of people have no clue what this means. And that's ok... so let me start off by defining macros. Macros are the main composition of food and include carbohydrates, proteins and fats. Each one of these play a different role in our bodies and we need all of them for a well balanced diet. When it comes to weight loss, the most important thing to understand is macronutrients.

## SO LET'S BREAK IT DOWN

**Carbohydrates** are what your body uses for fuel for day-to-day functions. These can come in healthy versions such as veggies, fruits, potatoes, grains and legumes, however, a lot of people tend to lean toward the not-so-healthy versions such as processed foods, breads, cookies, cakes, sweets etc. Healthy carbs are an essential part of digestion and keeping your blood sugars steady! Carbs can be simple carbs or complex carbs. The simple carbs are the carbs you see in fruits, veggies and sugar. These are typically easy to break down and you can either use them or store them quickly. Complex carbs come from rice, potatoes, quinoa etc. These take longer to break down and help you feel full. Carbs are either used as energy or stored as fat when the storage centers are full! So it is really important to focus on fibrous veggies and complex carbs.

**Proteins** build and maintain muscle. They also break down slowly, thus burning more calories during digestion. Ladies, don't let "muscle" scare you. You need muscle to help you lose weight and keep it off. Muscles increase and ramp up your metabolism as well: one pound of muscle can burn up to 20 calories per day at rest, whereas one pound of fat only burns 5 calories per day.

Your body cannot store protein so you are constantly having to replenish it. You get protein from real food but you can also supplement with protein powders, etc. When getting protein from food, you want to eat LEAN protein. 1 gram of protein equals 4 calories. Typically, you will want to get at least .8-1x your bodyweight in grams of protein. For example, if you weigh 200 lbs, you will want to get 160-200 grams of protein a day to maintain your muscles.

**Healthy fats** are also an essential part of any diet. Fats are actually very important in your hormonal balance as well as weight loss, but you have to choose "good fats." Good fats consist of avocado, olive oil, nuts, eggs, etc. 1 gram of fat is equal to 9 calories. Typically, you want your fat calories to be lower than the calories you receive from proteins and carbs. Eaten in moderation and in conjunction with the right amount of carbs on each particular day (high carb day vs. low carb day), they help your energy levels stay steady and keep you from feeling hungry.

Although tracking your macros is essential in hitting your goals, nutrition choices need to go beyond the basic IIFYM (if it fits your macros), and the numbers you need depend on what your goals are. Everyone has different goals and different body types and activity levels ... all these things affect what your macros should be on a day-to-day basis.

*With new research coming out about the benefits of intermittent fasting in terms of weight loss and overall health... the industry is beginning to take note. While this incredibly effective nutritional strategy has not yet become mainstream, it is becoming more and more popular as the results truly do speak for themselves.*

So why do you need to count your macros? Because it is so important when it comes to reaching your goals. Getting the right amount of carbohydrates, proteins, and fats in your diet is essential to meet your goals – whether you want to build muscle or lose weight – or both! Getting too much or too little of any macronutrient can mess with your metabolism, energy levels, muscle gains/losses, fat gains/losses, or hormone levels. Tracking your macronutrients is essentially tracking where your calories are coming from.

For years, the fitness industry's party line in terms of weight loss has been to restrict your calories and eat multiple small meals spread out throughout the day to keep your metabolism working all day long. That is, until recently. With new research coming out about the benefits of intermittent fasting in terms of weight loss and overall health... the industry is beginning to take note. While this incredibly effective nutritional strategy has not yet become mainstream, it is becoming more and more popular as the results truly do speak for themselves.

Because intermittent fasting is still relatively new on the scene, there is a lot of confusion about what it is and how to implement it effectively. Intermittent fasting is not a diet; it is an eating schedule. It says nothing about which foods you CAN eat, but rather WHEN you can eat. You are cycling between patterns of eating and fasting (not eating).

Your body is constantly in one of two states - fed or fasted. When you are in a "fed" state, your body is working hard to produce insulin to break down and digest food. However, in a "fasted" state, which is typically between 8-10 hours after the digestion process has stopped, your body is given a break from insulin production and is able to pull into your fat stores. Interesting enough, people rarely enter into a "fasted" state. We are taught to eat small meals regularly throughout the day which is keeping up in constant digestion. I'm here to tell you that this is not necessarily the right thing to do when wanting to keep/build lean calorie burning muscle while decreasing fat.

*We are taught to eat small meals regularly throughout the day which is keeping up in constant digestion. I'm here to tell you that this is not necessarily the right thing to do when wanting to keep/build lean calorie burning muscle while decreasing fat.*

When you practice intermittent fasting, you allow your body to de-stress from a constant production of insulin and your blood sugar can regulate itself. It reduces stress on your cells and organs, allowing them to heal naturally and re-group. Intermittent fasting also helps to normalize your hunger hormones! Studies show that this lifestyle actually increases your metabolic rate - causing you to burn more calories throughout the day.

There are several ways to follow an intermittent fasting lifestyle but the most common ways are either a once a week 24 hour fast, or the daily 16/8 protocol (this is what I follow).

Intermittent fasting has incredible benefits for those wanting to burn fat, increase their energy, and prevent illness. Using the 16/8 fasting protocol is incredibly sustainable and will give you the results you are looking for however, I would suggest having support from a nutritionist, trainer or doctor when you first begin this.

Read worksheet 7:2 on page 133 and keep somewhere you can easily access!

Since we addressed the most effective nutritional strategies for fat loss, let me now address the ever-controversial topic - calorie-restricted diets. Yes, these types of diets will get you results pretty quickly. However, let's dive into the long-term side effects of calorie restriction.

While living in a calorie deficit can yield weight loss (it always does), it is not the healthiest option. When you live in a calorie deficit for too long some of the long-term side effects include abnormal hormone fluctuations (including adrenal and thyroid), trouble concentrating and memory loss, weight loss plateau and a very slow metabolism, mineral deficiencies, and so much more. You will begin to burn muscle, and when that happens your metabolic rate decreases making it hard to lose fat. You may begin to feel like you can never get "toned" like you want even though you may be eating "healthy" and working out.

Please understand that a long-term calorie restricted diet is NOT the way to live your life. Your body needs fuel to burn fat.

Resources

Merriam-webster.com. (2018). Definition of ANXIETY. [online] Available at: https://www.merriam-webster.com/dictionary/anxiety [Accessed 8 Aug. 2018].

# Addressing Anxiety & Fear

What areas of your life do you feel anxious in?

What are the physical feelings of your anxiety?

What are a few ways you can cope with that anxiety rather than turning to food?

What does God say about your anxious thoughts? And how can you gain peace through this?

What fears do you have about your health journey?

List 5 ways to overcome those fears:

1.

2.

3.

4.

5.

List 5 support people in your life you can call when feeling anxious?

1.

2.

3.

4.

5.

# The Do's + Don'ts of Intermitent Fasting

## INTERMITTENT FASTING DON'TS

1.  Don't restrict your calories: Intermittent fasting is NOT a way to restrict your calories. Doing so has negative long-term effects on your metabolic rate, adrenal glands and overall health.

2.  Don't stress over WHEN your fasting window is: Don't worry about your times, worry about the number of hours you are fasting/eating.

3.  Don't stare at the clock counting down the minutes until you are able to eat: This will only make your fasting window absolutely miserable!

4.  Don't bite off more than you can chew with your fast: You DON'T have to hop into a 16 hour fast on day 1. It is totally fine to ease your way in!

5.  Don't feel like you have to start with breakfast: Lots of people don't want to eat breakfast at noon or 1pm. That's totally fine! But if you DO love breakfast foods, then by all means, have pancakes at noon! I do this often.

## INTERMITTENT FASTING DO'S

1.  Do eat ALL of your macros every day: It is important that you get ALL of your macros in each day to keep your metabolism functioning appropriately!

2.  Do allow for some flexibility in your fasting, for when life happens: Move your eating window around as needed. Don't worry too much about the times, just keep your fast at least 16 hours long and your feeding window no more than 8 hours long!

3.  Do stay busy during your fasting window: One of the greatest benefits of intermittent fasting is that you have time each day with no food prep or meals to worry about. Use that time wisely and focus your energy on staying busy!

4.  Do start off slow and extend your fasting window when you are ready. You can start with a 12 hour fasting window for a couple of days, then work your way up, adding an hour or two until you reach a 16 hour fasting window!

5.  Do eat whatever you want when you break your fast: You are a grown up. You can eat whatever you want (within a whole foods based diet) when you break your fast!

# Weekly Reflection

What were the biggest revelations and lessons learned this week?

What are you grateful for this past week?

List three positives of the week when it comes to your nutrition and exercise journey:

1.

2.

3.

List three things you would like to improve on next week.
What concrete actions can you take to work towards these?

1.

2.

3.

When did you catch yourself anxious this week? And how did you overcome it?

From 1-10, how do you feel you did this week?

What does Philippians 4:6-7 mean to you this week?

> "Be anxious for nothing, but in everything by prayer and supplication with thanksgiving let your requests be made known to God. And the peace of God which surpasses all comprehension, will guard your hearts and your minds in Christ Jesus." Philippians 4:6-7

How can you apply this verse moving forward on this journey?

How did you feel with the intermittent fast? What could you try next week to succeed again?

# WEEK SEVEN DEVOTIONS

Ephesians 3:16-19

[16] I pray that out of his glorious riches he may strengthen you with power through his Spirit in your inner being, [17] so that Christ may dwell in your hearts through faith. And I pray that you, being rooted and established in love, [18] may have power, together with all the Lord's holy people, to grasp how wide and long and high and deep is the love of Christ, [19] and to know this love that surpasses knowledge—that you may be filled to the measure of all the fullness of God.

*W*e all have different areas in our lives where lack of peace hits us, yet we all have areas that are peaceful. Remember in the last study where we shine our light is where we look or where we define what we want is where we see movement. In this case the same holds true, so you've looked at ways to lower anxiety, now let's identify where we have felt peace and emulate that in other areas of our lives.

**In your journal** list out what I call big rock areas in your life...those areas that take our time and energy. For instance: Spiritual Life, Husband, Children, Finances, Health, School, etc. Identify if you feel peace in any of these areas. Keep in mind, we will never feel peace 100% of the time in all areas, but rather, identify any measure of peace you might feel in one or numerous of these areas. If you don't have even a grain of peace in any area look back in your past and see if you can identify even a moment or an hour where you felt peace. Keep in mind, peaceful doesn't necessarily mean happiness or joyful. For instance, one of the most peace felt moments in my life was also the most heartbreaking to date. When my mother passed away I felt this peace overwhelm me that she was there in spirit, looking at the 30 or so people in the room all holding hands and praying as the life left her body. Sometimes peace is during sacred moments such as these and other times they are after a satisfying meal and good conversation with a friend where you feel safe, fulfilled and complete.

**Utilize your journal** while you **meditate** and think on the following:

What was I doing that I felt peace in my heart, soul and body?
What was different than today in that area? How did that peace feel?
So much of what we have been discussing ties together. Peace comes when we are not comparing ourselves to others, rather when we have a focus on our personal relationship with God and others. Where in your life do you need to let go and let God? **Pray** over this list, asking God to help you let these items go.

**Read** the following versus: **Proverbs 14:30, Ephesians 3: 16-20, Colossians 1:9-14 and 2:6-7; 2 Timothy 1:7; Psalms 139:11-12**

What do these verses say to me?

How does this relate to me finding peace?

Knowing God is there, that He is strengthening you, that He is loving you, that He is helping you find gratitude and can help you push out the darkness, how does this reassure you? How does this help you realize you cannot find peace by yourself? Knowing a great weight is lifted off us, how does this relate to what you are dealing with right now?

## Digging Deep

*Using the list you created, utilize your journal write out a prayer, asking God to remove the worry and anxiety associated with whatever you have going on in your life. Ask and you shall receive so be specific in asking God to remove this and fill you with His peace that passes all understanding. Once you have written this prayer, read it out loud. Writing and then reading out loud is powerful so don't skip that step! Shalom to you friends!*

How can I let go of my worries knowing God's got this?

If you struggle with meditating, sometimes music can help. Here are two suggestions: Celtic Psalms by Deirdre Nicole Neely is a great CD to play while meditating, particularly if you are just starting out and need something to fill the quiet.

Pandora has numerous stations – I really like Hawaiian Radio because come on, who can't relax when listening to music of the islands?

## Journal it!

_____

_____

_____

If you are in need of a workout plan or nutrition guidance, please jump in to my next virtual bootcamp at jennymire.com or take advantage of the full Think Fit Method portal at thinkfitmethod.com

# **MONDAY** - TRACK YOUR WORKOUT

Exercise: _____

*Rate how you feel*

| Before Workout: | 1 | 2 | 3 | 4 | 5 | 6 | 7 | 8 | 9 | 10 |
|---|---|---|---|---|---|---|---|---|---|---|

| During Workout: | 1 | 2 | 3 | 4 | 5 | 6 | 7 | 8 | 9 | 10 |
|---|---|---|---|---|---|---|---|---|---|---|

| After Workout: | 1 | 2 | 3 | 4 | 5 | 6 | 7 | 8 | 9 | 10 |
|---|---|---|---|---|---|---|---|---|---|---|

Total exercise time: _____   Approximate Calories Burned: _____

Water Goal (oz): _____   Water Consumed (oz): _____

*Today My Win Was:* _____
*Tomorrow I Will:* _____

# **TUESDAY** - TRACK YOUR WORKOUT

Exercise: _____

*Rate how you feel*

| Before Workout: | 1 | 2 | 3 | 4 | 5 | 6 | 7 | 8 | 9 | 10 |
|---|---|---|---|---|---|---|---|---|---|---|

| During Workout: | 1 | 2 | 3 | 4 | 5 | 6 | 7 | 8 | 9 | 10 |
|---|---|---|---|---|---|---|---|---|---|---|

| After Workout: | 1 | 2 | 3 | 4 | 5 | 6 | 7 | 8 | 9 | 10 |
|---|---|---|---|---|---|---|---|---|---|---|

Total exercise time: _____   Approximate Calories Burned: _____

Water Goal (oz): _____   Water Consumed (oz): _____

*Today My Win Was:* _____
*Tomorrow I Will:* _____

# WEDNESDAY - TRACK YOUR WORKOUT

Exercise: _____

## Rate how you feel

| Before Workout: | 1 | 2 | 3 | 4 | 5 | 6 | 7 | 8 | 9 | 10 |
|---|---|---|---|---|---|---|---|---|---|---|

| During Workout: | 1 | 2 | 3 | 4 | 5 | 6 | 7 | 8 | 9 | 10 |
|---|---|---|---|---|---|---|---|---|---|---|

| After Workout: | 1 | 2 | 3 | 4 | 5 | 6 | 7 | 8 | 9 | 10 |
|---|---|---|---|---|---|---|---|---|---|---|

Total exercise time: ☐          Approximate Calories Burned: ☐

Water Goal (oz): ☐          Water Consumed (oz): ☐

Today My Win Was: _____

Tomorrow I Will: _____

# THURSDAY - TRACK YOUR WORKOUT

Exercise: _____

## Rate how you feel

| Before Workout: | 1 | 2 | 3 | 4 | 5 | 6 | 7 | 8 | 9 | 10 |
|---|---|---|---|---|---|---|---|---|---|---|

| During Workout: | 1 | 2 | 3 | 4 | 5 | 6 | 7 | 8 | 9 | 10 |
|---|---|---|---|---|---|---|---|---|---|---|

| After Workout: | 1 | 2 | 3 | 4 | 5 | 6 | 7 | 8 | 9 | 10 |
|---|---|---|---|---|---|---|---|---|---|---|

Total exercise time: ☐          Approximate Calories Burned: ☐

Water Goal (oz): ☐          Water Consumed (oz): ☐

Today My Win Was: _____

Tomorrow I Will: _____

# **FRIDAY** - TRACK YOUR WORKOUT

Exercise: _____

*Rate how you feel*

| Before Workout: | 1 | 2 | 3 | 4 | 5 | 6 | 7 | 8 | 9 | 10 |
|---|---|---|---|---|---|---|---|---|---|---|

| During Workout: | 1 | 2 | 3 | 4 | 5 | 6 | 7 | 8 | 9 | 10 |
|---|---|---|---|---|---|---|---|---|---|---|

| After Workout: | 1 | 2 | 3 | 4 | 5 | 6 | 7 | 8 | 9 | 10 |
|---|---|---|---|---|---|---|---|---|---|---|

Total exercise time: _____    Approximate Calories Burned: _____

Water Goal (oz): _____        Water Consumed (oz): _____

*Today My Win Was:* _____

*Tomorrow I Will:* _____

# **WEEKEND** - TRACK YOUR WORKOUT

Exercise: _____

*Rate how you feel*

| Before Workout: | 1 | 2 | 3 | 4 | 5 | 6 | 7 | 8 | 9 | 10 |
|---|---|---|---|---|---|---|---|---|---|---|

| During Workout: | 1 | 2 | 3 | 4 | 5 | 6 | 7 | 8 | 9 | 10 |
|---|---|---|---|---|---|---|---|---|---|---|

| After Workout: | 1 | 2 | 3 | 4 | 5 | 6 | 7 | 8 | 9 | 10 |
|---|---|---|---|---|---|---|---|---|---|---|

Total exercise time: _____    Approximate Calories Burned: _____

Water Goal (oz): _____        Water Consumed (oz): _____

*Today My Win Was:* _____

*Tomorrow I Will:* _____

## LETTING GO OF GUILT & SHAME + YOU'VE CONQUERED

8

# WEEK EIGHT

ou've CONQUERED! We are on the last week, friend! Can you believe it? Before we start in on letting go of past guilt and shame, I want you to close your eyes – RIGHT NOW – and think about the past 7 weeks on your health journey. Think about each good choice you've made on this journey. Think about how far you have really come. Do this for 2-3 minutes and then move on to worksheet 8:1.

You have come so far and it's time to relish in that but there may be one last thing weighing you down... and that is guilt/shame.

Guilt is a powerful thing and can paralyze us in our steps. Seriously, it can PARALYZE us. We freeze. We don't know what to do next because we feel so guilty.

Am I right?
Have you ever felt this way?
I know I have.

> *"Therefore, having been justified by faith, we have peace with God through our Lord Jesus Christ, through whom also we have obtained our introduction by faith into this grace in which we stand; and we exalt in hope of the glory of God. And not only this, but we also exult in our tribulations, knowing that tribulation brings about perseverance; and perseverance, proven character; and proven character, hope; and hope does not disappoint, because the love of God has been poured out within our hearts through the Holy Spirit who was given to us."*
> *Romans 5: 1-5*

Friends, we are saved through faith. God calls us to repent and release that guilt and shame to Him and He will lift it off our shoulders. Once you repent and have moved on, don't let Satan have a strong hold on you through guilt and shame. If you continue to let these things haunt you, then Satan wins. He will hold you back from taking this step into a life of freedom.

*"For the sorrow that is according to the will of God produces a repentance without regret, leading to salvation, but the sorrow of the world produces death."* 2 Corinthians 4:15

So let go.

Release it to Jesus.

Step into the freedom of Christ and who He has called you to be.

*"Therefore there is now no condemnation for those who are in Christ Jesus."* Romans 8:1

Throughout this journey, my hope and prayer that if you only got one thing out of it, it would be to believe that YOU ARE WORTH IT. Your life and your health matters.

Now, you have learned SO MUCH the past 7 weeks in this program but how do you make this a lifestyle? The biggest thing I want you to continue to do is to go back to these worksheets week in and week out. Continue to tell yourself that you are worth it. That you are beautiful. That you CAN do this. Because guess what? YOU CAN DO THIS. You are very capable of living this healthy lifestyle. You are very capable of continuing to utilize the tools you have learned. You are very capable to continue eating whole foods. And what better way to show yourself that you are worth it than to continue what you've learned?!

And as you continue this healthy lifestyle, I challenge you to start talking to your family members about it. Start encouraging those around you to make healthy choices as well. Be an example of health to those you run into day in and out. Because they are worth it, too.

And as we wrap up, there is a song I just love and I want to share part of it with you...

FEAR IS A LIAR
by Zach Williams

"When he told you you're not good enough
When he told you you're not right
When he told you you're not strong enough
To put up a good fight
When he told you you're not worthy
When he told you you're not loved
When he told you you're not beautiful
That you'll never be enough
- - - - -
Fear, he is a liar
He will take your breath
Stop you in your steps
Fear he is a liar
He will rob your rest
Steal your happiness
Cast your fear in the fire
'Cause fear he is a liar"

Don't let fear hold you back anymore. Fear is a liar. Face it head on and let's take the step into the new you. Be proud! Be very proud of how far you have come the past 8 weeks! Cheers to a NEW YOU!

Resources
Fear Is A Liar (Lyrics) | Zach Williams. (2018). Retrieved from http://zachwilliamsmusic.com/fear-is-a-liar-lyrics/

# Your Think Fit Method Experience

IT'S TIME TO JOURNAL ABOUT THIS THINK FIT METHOD EXPERIENCE.

What 3 things did you find hard during this program?

1.

2.

3.

What are 3 learning points that will help you continue to move forward?

1.

2.

3.

What are 3 things you really liked about this process?

1.

2.

3.

What is the best moment you've had in your health journey over the last couple months?

Who are 2-3 people in your LIFE that would benefit from Think Fit Method that you could share this opportunity with and have them start at thinkfitmethod.com?

# Weekly Reflection

What were the biggest revelations and lessons learned this week?

What are you grateful for this past week?

List three positives of the week when it comes to your nutrition and exercise journey:

1.

2.

3.

List three things you would like to improve on next week.
What concrete actions can you take to work towards these?

1.

2.

3.

When did you show yourself you are worth it this week?
List as many as applicable:

From 1-10, how do you feel you did this week?

What does Romans 8:1 mean to you this week?

*"Therefore there is now no condemnation for those who are in Christ Jesus."*

*Romans 8:1*

How can you apply this verse moving forward on this journey?

How do you plan to continue living your best healthy life after this week? What's next?

# WEEK EIGHT DEVOTIONS

Hebrews 10:19-22

[19] Therefore, brothers and sisters, since we have confidence to enter the Most Holy Place by the blood of Jesus, [20] by a new and living way opened for us through the curtain, that is, his body, [21] and since we have a great priest over the house of God, [22] let us draw near to God with a sincere heart and with the full assurance that faith brings, having our hearts sprinkled to cleanse us from a guilty conscience and having our bodies washed with pure water.

Throughout these last 7 weeks my hope and prayer from this study was to help you see the overwhelming love God has for you and how this love that we are not humanly capable of is in us!! This love allows us to love our neighbors as ourselves and provides a peace beyond understanding! Part of finding peace is understanding the difference between guilt and shame and letting go of those feelings that are getting in the way of our relationship with God and from being all who we are meant to be!

Let's take a moment to understand guilt and shame. Brene' Brown, a well-known researcher on shame, provides the following information on her blog:

> "I believe there is a profound difference between shame and guilt. I believe guilt is adaptive and helpful – it's holding something we've done or failed to do up against our values and feeling psychological discomfort. I define shame as the intensely painful feeling or experience of believing that we are flawed and therefore unworthy of love and belonging – something we've experienced, done, or failed to do makes us unworthy of connection."

**Read Hebrews 10:19-25**
God can and will cleanse us from guilt and shame. What are you holding onto right now that you feel guilty about or that has led to shame? Make a list, but don't focus on how awful this feels, but rather find a close trusted friend and review this list with them. (You may find the later part of these verses to be true as your friend may need the same support). Some will be about you, others may involve other people who you need to forgive or whom you need to ask forgiveness from. Sometimes it is wise to approach others and ask for forgiveness and other times because it may cause more harm, it's best to write a letter and burn it. Work with this trusted friend or a therapist to work through this list. Then **pray** asking God to take the burden from you and LET IT GO my friend!! LET IT GO!

The funny thing about guilt is it can be helpful; however, when we let it turn into shame, then we must look at why we are doing what we are doing. Guilt and shame tie directly to forgiveness. As part of my master's program I took a class on forgiveness and was surprised because as I started to investigate all the people I felt I needed to forgive and or ask forgiveness from, the biggest one was myself. How freeing this was knowing that God was able (I wasn't) to take this guilt and shame away from me! I had to be aware of it and work to let it go and let me tell you "it" had scratch marks all over it by the time I let it go at the foot of the cross! Where do you need to forgive yourself? Take some time to **meditate** and **journal** on this question.

Guilt and shame lie heavily in most health, weight loss and eating journeys. Roth (2011) states "Overeating was my way to punish and shame myself; each time I gained weight, each time I failed at a diet, I proved to myself that my deepest fear was true. I was pathetic and doomed, and I didn't deserve to live" (p. 23). Now for some of us, this statement hits the bullseye while others we have not gotten to the point where we felt we didn't deserve to live. The point here is that we all struggle with shame and shame my friends is usually associated to all the things we have been discussing. My prayer is we all stop the cycle of guilt leading to shame leading to continued self-sabotage. It's a vicious cycle, but we have the ability, with God to STOP the cycle!

*Digging Deep*

*Take the time to read The Gifts of Imperfection: Letting Go of Who You Think You're Supposed to Be and Embrace Who You Are by Brene' Brown, Ph.D. L.M.S.W. and do the exercises she suggests. Find a group of people who are on a health journey such as yourself and ask them to read it and discuss with you. Having a group of people to support you and help you through this process is critical and enriches your life!*

**Read John 3:16** This verse is the cornerstone of the Christian faith and one that we can sometimes overlook. Think about this...we are SO WORTHY that God came to earth as a human to experience all the things we experience. He took time with his Father, prayed, meditated, spent time with a tribe that supported him (the disciples) and frankly let him down numerous times, struggled with temptation, self-doubt (**Matthew 26:39**) and then went through terrible physical pain where he endured. Why? Because HE LOVES YOU! My friends, I pray you continue to grow in your relationship with our heavenly Father and that you experience God in a whole new way as you continue your health journey! Shalom!

Resources

Brown, B. 2013. Shame v. Guilt. https://brenebrown.com/blog/2013/01/14/shame-v.guilt/
Roth, G. (2011). Women, food and God. New York: Scribner.

# Journal it!

_____

_____

_____

_____

_____

_____

_____

_____

_____

_____

_____

_____

_____

_____

_____

_____

_____

_____

_____

If you are in need of a workout plan or nutrition guidance, please jump in to my next virtual bootcamp at jennymire.com or take advantage of the full Think Fit Method portal at thinkfitmethod.com

# **MONDAY** - TRACK YOUR WORKOUT

Exercise: _____

*Rate how you feel*

| Before Workout: | 1 | 2 | 3 | 4 | 5 | 6 | 7 | 8 | 9 | 10 |
|---|---|---|---|---|---|---|---|---|---|---|

| During Workout: | 1 | 2 | 3 | 4 | 5 | 6 | 7 | 8 | 9 | 10 |
|---|---|---|---|---|---|---|---|---|---|---|

| After Workout: | 1 | 2 | 3 | 4 | 5 | 6 | 7 | 8 | 9 | 10 |
|---|---|---|---|---|---|---|---|---|---|---|

Total exercise time: _____    Approximate Calories Burned: _____

Water Goal (oz): _____        Water Consumed (oz): _____

*Today My Win Was:* _____
*Tomorrow I Will:* _____

# **TUESDAY** - TRACK YOUR WORKOUT

Exercise: _____

*Rate how you feel*

| Before Workout: | 1 | 2 | 3 | 4 | 5 | 6 | 7 | 8 | 9 | 10 |
|---|---|---|---|---|---|---|---|---|---|---|

| During Workout: | 1 | 2 | 3 | 4 | 5 | 6 | 7 | 8 | 9 | 10 |
|---|---|---|---|---|---|---|---|---|---|---|

| After Workout: | 1 | 2 | 3 | 4 | 5 | 6 | 7 | 8 | 9 | 10 |
|---|---|---|---|---|---|---|---|---|---|---|

Total exercise time: _____    Approximate Calories Burned: _____

Water Goal (oz): _____        Water Consumed (oz): _____

*Today My Win Was:* _____
*Tomorrow I Will:* _____

# WEDNESDAY - TRACK YOUR WORKOUT

Exercise: _____

## Rate how you feel

| Before Workout: | 1 | 2 | 3 | 4 | 5 | 6 | 7 | 8 | 9 | 10 |
|---|---|---|---|---|---|---|---|---|---|---|

| During Workout: | 1 | 2 | 3 | 4 | 5 | 6 | 7 | 8 | 9 | 10 |
|---|---|---|---|---|---|---|---|---|---|---|

| After Workout: | 1 | 2 | 3 | 4 | 5 | 6 | 7 | 8 | 9 | 10 |
|---|---|---|---|---|---|---|---|---|---|---|

Total exercise time: _____  Approximate Calories Burned: _____

Water Goal (oz): _____  Water Consumed (oz): _____

Today My Win Was: _____

Tomorrow I Will: _____

# THURSDAY - TRACK YOUR WORKOUT

Exercise: _____

## Rate how you feel

| Before Workout: | 1 | 2 | 3 | 4 | 5 | 6 | 7 | 8 | 9 | 10 |
|---|---|---|---|---|---|---|---|---|---|---|

| During Workout: | 1 | 2 | 3 | 4 | 5 | 6 | 7 | 8 | 9 | 10 |
|---|---|---|---|---|---|---|---|---|---|---|

| After Workout: | 1 | 2 | 3 | 4 | 5 | 6 | 7 | 8 | 9 | 10 |
|---|---|---|---|---|---|---|---|---|---|---|

Total exercise time: _____  Approximate Calories Burned: _____

Water Goal (oz): _____  Water Consumed (oz): _____

Today My Win Was: _____

Tomorrow I Will: _____

# FRIDAY - TRACK YOUR WORKOUT

Exercise: _____

## Rate how you feel

| Before Workout: | 1 | 2 | 3 | 4 | 5 | 6 | 7 | 8 | 9 | 10 |
|---|---|---|---|---|---|---|---|---|---|---|
| During Workout: | 1 | 2 | 3 | 4 | 5 | 6 | 7 | 8 | 9 | 10 |
| After Workout: | 1 | 2 | 3 | 4 | 5 | 6 | 7 | 8 | 9 | 10 |

Total exercise time: _____  Approximate Calories Burned: _____

Water Goal (oz): _____  Water Consumed (oz): _____

Today My Win Was: _____
Tomorrow I Will: _____

# WEEKEND - TRACK YOUR WORKOUT

Exercise: _____

## Rate how you feel

| Before Workout: | 1 | 2 | 3 | 4 | 5 | 6 | 7 | 8 | 9 | 10 |
|---|---|---|---|---|---|---|---|---|---|---|
| During Workout: | 1 | 2 | 3 | 4 | 5 | 6 | 7 | 8 | 9 | 10 |
| After Workout: | 1 | 2 | 3 | 4 | 5 | 6 | 7 | 8 | 9 | 10 |

Total exercise time: _____  Approximate Calories Burned: _____

Water Goal (oz): _____  Water Consumed (oz): _____

Today My Win Was: _____
Tomorrow I Will: _____

# What's Next

As we wrap up our time in Think Fit Journal & Devotion, I'm sure you are thinking "what's next"?

This is a very important thing to process through as you continue your wellness journey. The next step would be learning intentional nutrition and how to choose foods that will fuel your body along with strategic exercise.

Please check out *www.jennymire.com* for all your health and wellness needs.

# ABOUT JENNY

My name is Jenny Mire and I am a Certified Personal Trainer with my college degree in the Education and Counseling fields. I understand from personal experience that it is hard to find the motivation to lose weight on your own. I understand the struggles of food addiction and emotional eating. I understand the struggles of life and being busy. That is why I have made it my mission to teach other women what I have learned over the years – that they CAN do it with the proper tools.

Thank you for trusting me as your trainer and fitness coach! I am excited to help you start (or continue) on your journey to health. Please take a minute to learn a little more about me and my journey below. I have NOT always been "fit" or "in shape." My journey was a difficult one – but one I am proud of. And I hope I can inspire YOU to make the change, too.

I am a daughter of the one true God, a wife, a mom of three, a sister, a friend, and today I know myself better than I ever have. Because of this, I am able to share my passion, knowledge and experience with those whose paths cross mine. I have never been more excited about the call on my life to help others find the healthy life they desire.

My story isn't unlike many of yours. I was not always healthy, or active. I lacked confidence in myself, and for a long time, I also lacked the belief that I needed to have in myself to change my health for the better. I was not always confident. I didn't view myself as "worth it." I was an emotional eater. I hated exercise. I dabbled in "fads" and short term windows of motivation offered me some success, but ultimately my heart wasn't in it. I didn't have the right outlook or understanding of what it truly meant to treat my body as a temple and to honor the one who created it. Saving my calories all day for Cold Stone ice cream and Subway sandwiches (true story) didn't lead to anything but a body that was hungry for nutrients and a mind that knew this wasn't the answer. I was self sabotaging.

Growing up, I was never the "athletic" type. I carried a little extra weight and I did not care to be "healthy." My childhood was one of staying out of the spotlight - I was not the "popular" girl in school. I kept to myself most of the time, but luckily, God brought a young boy into my life who loved me for me. I married my high school sweetheart while obtaining my degree in Education and Counseling, Educational, and Developmental Psychology. After years of letting myself go, enduring struggles, miscarriage and depression, my husband and I had our first daughter. Immediately following her delivery in 2007, I was diagnosed with postpartum depression. And within a month, I had to have my gallbladder removed. Needless to say, I was a wreck. This wasn't the picture of life I thought I would have.

Sixteen months later we had our second daughter. I started having migraines and was constantly tired. The excess weight was dragging me down and I continued to struggle with bouts of depression that led me to emotional eating. I tried exercise videos and dieting but nothing seemed to work as I slipped deeper into depression. The years following, I was good at faking it. I lost some of the baby weight but my body hurt. I would cry out to God and pray that something in me would change. Meanwhile, two years later, I became pregnant with my third girl. I had a very rough pregnancy, being on bed rest and gaining over 60 lbs. We had our baby girl in Spring of 2011 and one year later something inside me snapped. I was sick of being overweight and tired. I was tired of the sadness and lack of energy I had. I was tired of the headaches. I was tired of being so self-conscious about everything I wore and everything I did.

I can't pinpoint the exact moment, but it happened, and I knew it was time to dig in and put in the work to change my life. It started with motivation, which inspired me to study and research. I wrestled with God about my worth and this propelled me to follow through and put in the work. I fell in love with weight lifting - something I was never taught to do as a woman. I started researching and understanding nutrition and my body changed, but my mind change, too. I began to lean out - FINALLY - without doing hours upon hours of cardio. As my body began to change, my self image began to change. I began to love myself. Even though I still had a "ways to go" with weight loss, I finally began to see myself as worth it. And as my body continued to change, the emotional eating stopped. I implemented tools (from my mental health background and schooling) and allowed God to do a work in my life that helped when I found myself sinking back into depression and anxiety that led to emotional eating along my journey. I truly began to see myself the way that God intended - a child of the King. Finally able to see my LIFE as worth it. To fuel my body the way I was supposed to. To work through my own mental health struggles. My life changed.

In 2014, at the same time I was selling my social work agency, I went back to school and studied at the International Sports Science Association to obtain my certificate in personal training, because I felt a strong desire to start helping women the way I wish I would have had help in the beginning. I felt the stir of helping lift up others (by giving them the tools they needed) become an igniting passion in myself. That winter, I purchased a local gym where I could share my passion and knowledge with my community and from there I continued to invest in this field and grow in my knowledge of health, nutrition and overall wellness. I took things to the next level when I began online trainings and bootcamps that could help women I couldn't physically reach. And my heart for working with people grew even more, and still does.

I realize now more than ever that healthy living starts inside- we have to have our emotional health in check to truly thrive, and I am a champion for that above all else. My three girls continue to be the inspiration that brought me to the place I am now. I am healthy, fueled and strong. I am imperfect but I am equipped and I know that motivation sometimes runs out but consistency pays off. And that is likely why my story and yours are similar. Each one of us has come to a place where we want to treat our body well, by feeding and training well for life. We all have our "reason(s)" and we push because we are capable.

Today I am here: healthier and fuller and finally holding on to the needed knowledge and personal experience necessary to continue to treat my body as God would have me, starting with my head and heart and letting that be the catalyst for my overall health. Training hard, finding balance and eating to fuel my body rather than mistreat it.

I'm here with an open heart and a true desire to be your biggest cheerleader and champion for you. We are all capable of living healthy lives to the fullest and I believe God has equipped me to be a source of encouragement and beyond for those who He brings my way. My passion lies in running my online fitness bootcamps with women just like you and me, all over the world. My mission is to empower and teach other women how to look and feel their best no matter what the age. And I want YOU to know your worth. That is why I have created the Think Fit Method™.

In the fall of 2017, after years of running fat loss virtual bootcamps and training women in person at my gym, I found there was a BIGGER struggle to losing weight than just 'knowing' what to do. I found that the bigger struggle starts in the mind. I, personally, continued to struggle with binging, self sabotaging myself and feeling guilty around having a "treat." I spent many days in prayer about what to do... and what was next. I knew that God put me in this position to help women because that is His plan for me.

In September of 2017, I was on a flight back home after an amazing health conference just reflecting and praying. Then it struck me, women LIKE ME need a program to heal their MIND before healing their bodies physically. It starts in the MIND first. And the biggest hurdle is believing that YOU ARE WORTH IT! At that moment, Think Fit Method was born. The Lord has been with me since, developing this whole program.

The Think Fit Method is a program designed to help you view your WORTH, heal your MIND, and get you FIT. There is a link between your weight and your mental health and vice versa. One of the biggest things in your health and fitness journey, whether you are trying to lose weight or not, is shifting your mindset. In order to change our outside we must FIRST change our inside. For more about what I offer please head to *jennymire.com* and *thinkfitmethod.com*

*Jenny*

## ABOUT DEBBIE

Debbie Heiser, M.A. is in love with Jesus, her husband of 26 years, Brent and her adult son Zach! She has been blessed to have spent over 27 years in leadership capacities with international, domestic, and small businesses and in numerous volunteer roles throughout her life. She had the fortunate opportunity to spend 9 years as a volunteer High School and Post High School Youth Pastor loving on young people and helping them experience God. She started Three Vines Consulting and Leadership Development working with individuals and organizations to develop leadership and business or life strategy. She is stepping into her calling, speaking, writing and coaching others and loving every minute of it! Her passion is helping people find their calling in life and with God's guidance, put practices and plans in place to lean into their purpose.